RICHMOND

1   Richmond: Cricket on the Green

British Cities and Towns

RICHMOND

From Kew Green to Ham Common

Kathleen Courlander

London
B. T. BATSFORD LTD

Our lesson is, that there are two Richmonds, one in Surrey and one in
Yorkshire, and that mine is the Surrey Richmond.

CHARLES DICKENS, *Great Expectations*

First Published, 1953

Printed and bound in Great Britain by Jarrold and Sons Ltd.
London and Norwich for the Publishers
B. T. BATSFORD LTD.,
4 Fitzhardinge Street, Portman Square, London, W.1

CONTENTS

CONTENTS

ACKNOWLEDGMENT

FIGURE 33 is reproduced by Gracious Permission of H.M. The Queen, from the original in the Royal Collection at Windsor Castle.

The Author and Publishers wish to thank the following whose photographs appear in this book:

The Ashmolean Museum, for fig. 4; Donovan E. H. Box, for figs. 15, 29, 35 and 37; J. Allan Cash, F.R.P.S., for figs. 7 and 34; *Country Life*, for fig. 31; The Fitzwilliam Museum, Cambridge, for fig. 10; A. F. Kersting, F.R.P.S., for figs. 3, 8, 9, 13, 14, 16–19, 21–24, 26–28, 30, 38–44 and 47–51; Lensart, for figs. 1 and 25; Richmond Public Libraries Committee, for figs. 2, 6, 11, 12 and 32; John H. Stone, for fig. 36; the Trustees of the Tate Gallery, for fig. 5; the Topical Press Agency Ltd., for fig. 20.

Figures 45 and 46 are from the Publishers' collection.

The Author also wishes to thank Mr. Gilbert Turner, F.L.A., Chief Librarian of Richmond Public Library and his staff for their assistance during her months of research, and to acknowledge the help she has received from many local residents.

LIST OF ILLUSTRATIONS

LIST OF ILLUSTRATIONS

2   A View of Henry VII Old Palace at Richmond (1742)
From an engraving after W. Shaftoe

3   Richmond: Old Palace and Gate House (*c.* 1500)

4 Richmond Palace from the River in 1562

From the drawing by Anthonis van den Wyngaerde

Chapter I

CREATION OF ROYAL MANOR

Wyngaerde—Topographical Aspects—Norman Days—The Belet Family—
Chaucer—Richard II—The Carthusian Monastery—"Rules of Customes"

I

IT may have been in the late spring or in the early summer of the year 1557 that Anthonis van den Wyngaerde, topographical draughtsman of Flemish origin, arrived with his sketching materials in the Royal manor of Richmond. It is believed that he served King Philip II of Spain, husband of Queen Mary I of England, as an official artist and he sketched the places his patrons visited, as in modern times photographers accompany members of the Royal Family on overseas tours. His views of Dover, London and the Royal Palaces of Greenwich, Whitehall, Hampton Court, Oatlands and Richmond are in the Sutherland Collection at the Ashmolean Museum, Oxford, and they rank among the earliest naturalistic topographical drawings of Britain in existence.

Philip II returned to England on his second visit in March 1557, and Wyngaerde, in Richmond some weeks later as his drawings indicate, saw the little village on the Thames, its life focused on the Tudor palace, golden and gleaming with its promise of high summer, its trees breaking into tender leaf, the hawthorn bushes, like the Royal servants, wearing white and green liveries, the swift, clean river gemmed with borders of turquoise forget-me-nots and amber kingcups. "Shene", they had called the place in olden days, and indeed, part of the Royal manor was still known by its ancient name, and "shene", a word beloved by poets, described its shining.

The artist was rowed to the opposite bank, to the meadows of Twickenham in Middlesex, and from this site he sketched the Palace, delineating its attractive, unusual façade, the walls near the river's brink, dangerously so for their permanence(4). It is interesting to compare the site of Richmond Palace in this drawing with

15

a contemporary one by Wyngaerde of Hampton Court, and note the relative situations of the two buildings to the Thames.

The Privy Lodgings, three storeys high, their stonework bright in the morning sun, intersected by tiers of oriel windows, were capped with octagonal turrets, crowned by lead cupolas. Each cupola had a weather-vane; he saw a medley of these vanes, flashing darts of light as they moved in the breeze, their gilding a characteristic of Royal Tudor roofs. His eyes followed the sweep of the precincts—the Great Orchard at the north-west boundary of the Palace, containing a neat, low woodyard building. The windows on the other side of the Privy apartments overlooked a garden, its beds laid out to resemble ribbon knots.

Garden and orchards were directed by the Lovell family. Thomas Lovell had been transferred from Greenwich by Henry VIII and his sons and grandsons were associated with Richmond Palace grounds throughout the Tudor dynasty. Thomas had had "green fingers" and the grapes, apples, peaches and damsons, the flowers for the distilling of sweet waters, and the salad herbs he grew in the mild Thames Valley air, had been welcomed by the Royal Family when they resided in other palaces.

Beyond the Privy Gardens lay the deserted Convent of the Observant Friars, its cloisters extending to a Gothic chapel. Then came the undulating, wooded hill, where only a few buildings emerged through the trees. The river curved, was looped like a ribbon so that to Wyngaerde, the Monastery of Syon on the Middlesex bank, appeared to be slightly behind the Palace. Looking across the clear landscape, he jotted down the names of the places he could see; to the right he indicated the spire of Old St. Paul's Cathedral in London. He delineated small craft plying up and down the Thames, and a boat laden with cargo was pulled by a team of men, who bent beneath the strain of their burden as they tugged the rope which was fastened to the vessel's mast.

Wyngaerde recrossed the Thames and went to the Green, and here he drew another aspect of the Palace, the principal gate-house, the Chapel Royal and the Great Hall, domestic offices nestling around it. Two long galleries extended for about two hundred yards from the Privy Lodgings to a tennis court; they ran parallel with the Convent of the Observant Friars and were a novel feature of the Palace. The upper one was roofed, the lower one had a tiled floor and here the Lovells had their potting-sheds. Beyond the Middle Court arose a canted or round tower with one hundred and twenty steps, galleries connecting it with the Privy Lodgings.

The apartments of some of the principal officers of the Household were arranged round the Great Court, and the Gentlemen of the Bedchamber were allotted lodgings here. They included Robert Cotton, who, formerly, had held the onerous position of "Officer of THE Remooving Wardroppe of Bedds unto Queen Marie." This was a difficult appointment for every few days when the Court moved to another palace, this official had to commandeer carts from the local people to transport baggage.

Cotton's story is recorded on the brass, the oldest memorial in the Richmond Parish Church, where his effigy and those of his wife and eight children are outlined above the inscription which describes how, after Queen Mary's death, "againe he became an Officer of THE Wardroppe, wher he served HER Mat^{ie} that now is Queene Elizabeth, many yeres And dyed Yeoma of the same Office . . ."

One morning in March, shortly before Wyngaerde went to Richmond, Strype tells us that the Princess Elizabeth, who was then at Somerset House, London, "took her horse and rode to the Palace of Shene with a goodly company of lords, knights and gentlemen". Probably the visit was made in connection with King Philip's return, an event which restored the Queen to cheerfulness and caused an interval of gaiety in the dismal routine of the Court. But the brilliant entertainments that Mary had organised to amuse her bridegroom at Richmond during the happy days of her honeymoon were not revived. Only two years previously Elizabeth, a prisoner on her way from the Tower of London to Woodstock, had passed a night in the Palace, when she had feared she was doomed to die.

2

Wyngaerde made many sketches at Richmond, but he did not complete his drawings immediately and he may have accompanied his patron when Philip left England abruptly, an angry, disappointed man, for he had failed to obtain the support he sought in his campaign against France. They remained unfinished until he was working in Spain, and in that land of violent contrasts, of brilliant, exotic foliage, of tiled patios, of sombre stone mansions, of intense sunlight and dark shadows, one day, perhaps, he thought of the Royal manor by the Thames, where pearl clouds swept low across a blue-grey sky, and the Palace emerged, rose-red and gilt-tipped, from its garland of trees.

He tinted his pen-and-ink drawings and today, as we examine the oblong sheets he used, we find that his rose-red has faded to pale coral, his vivid green to jade. He signed and dated one of them: "Anty van den Wyngaerde *fecit ad Vivum* A. A° 1562", and inscribed both with the word "Richemont". The spelling of the place with the fertile hill varied since its new appellation had been grafted on to ancient Shene, some sixty odd years previously by Henry VII.

When Wyngaerde drew Richmond Palace from the Green, he left an immense heritage to the Royal manor, for his drawing is the only existing representation of the building from that aspect. According to the custom of his period, he may have added one or two picturesque details which were not there, and in his drawing the Wardrobe is not as near the Archway as we see it today.

The Green extended to the Palace walls and sheep grazed, but it was forbidden pasture for hogs or geese and tenants who defied this regulation, were prosecuted heavily. In front of the main gate archers practised with bows and arrows, watched by one or two spectators.

He inserted gabled, half-timbered, tall chimneyed houses in the immediate vicinity, their dimensions dwarfed by the Palace, their doors opening on to the Green. He may have lodged in one of these dwellings for accommodation in the Palace was limited, and when King Philip came to Richmond, the local people were pressed to take his retinue into their own homes. Some agreed, although unwillingly, for the haughty Spaniards were trying lodgers, con-temptuous of simple English ways. The records of the Court Leet at Kingston-upon-Thames, prove that Robert Rutter, Thomas Dennys, William Pate and Harman Gullson of Richmond were each fined one shilling for refusing to give hospitality to the "liege subjects of the King and Queen" and John Amersham of the same place had such a strong argument with the constable of the manor about the matter, that he was charged three shillings and fourpence.

If the artist had changed his position and made additional sketches of the landscape—this time with his back to the Palace, he would have seen a few more houses and cottages flanking the Green, for fifty years later, these were described as old buildings in the Court Rolls of the manor. The Green unrolled its emerald acres like a great carpet as it converged into waste or common land in the direction of *Kayhough*, as the hamlet of Kew had been described in Henry VII's time. At the end of the Tudor dynasty the scribes simplified it to *Koo*; the name derived from the fact that the place had a quay, the *hough* indicating that the land near the river was low.

North-west of the Palace stood the Carthusian monastery, the House of Jesus of Bethlehem, founded by Henry V to expiate, as Shakespeare wove into the King's prayer on the eve of the Battle of Agincourt, "the wrong my father did in compassing the crown". It had been adapted as a secular residence after the monks had surrendered it to Henry VIII during the Reformation, but Queen Mary had recalled them, although they had had to wait until the Duchess of Somerset, who lived there, had been bribed to move to a finer dwelling. Then the monks had adjusted the building swiftly to their needs, Father Chauncy acting as prior. But with the decline of the Queen's health, her failure to produce the heir whose birth would have stabilised their position, their future was precarious. Sensing the possibility of a second upheaval, they looked apprehensively at the deserted Convent of the Observant Friars. The friars, who had been welcomed there by Henry VII, had been driven from their tranquil cloisters by his son.

3

The Green was linked with Great, Common or London Street by alleys and one of the oldest was Brewers Lane. On the other side of Great Street, a turning led to the Parish Church of St. Mary Magdalene built in Henry VII's reign. The Privy Purse accounted for the King's donations— "to the parish preste of Richemont for and towards the beloding of ther church", and the items totalled thirty-eight pounds, six shillings and eightpence.

A rough bridle-track, called a "worple", was the main thorough-fare from the church to the Hill summit; the manor was dotted with worples which the ploughmen were compelled to leave when they made their furrows. Regulations for their maintenance were arbi-trary, and tenants were fined heavily if they disregarded them, a process which continued through the centuries, until the fields were covered with houses and the worples became streets. Today only one street—Worple Way—is a reminder of the time when the locality was punctuated by these tracks.

A worple led to the Fryers Style at the top of the Hill, a well-known landmark, mentioned early in the Court Rolls, and which, traditionally, acquired its name because the friars were often seen there. They paused to gaze at the view, down the slopes of the common or waste land, where the Thames, a glittering silver snake with golden spots, coiled into the lavender-blue mists of the distant heights. On a clear day, a small, dark speck was distinct, an excit-ing, historic spot, for it was the Round Tower of Windsor Castle. The friars have gone, the stile has vanished, but the tradition is remembered by Friars Stile Road.

There was another track, still nameless, which extended from the Hill to Great Street and branched half-way down, to the river and the ferry. There were no bridges in the district and the ferrymen car-ried passengers from Richmond to Twickenham, or rowed them up and down the Thames. The ferry belonged to the Sovereign as Lord of the Royal manor, and it was leased for the annual rent of thirteen shillings and fourpence, usually to a retainer who had retired from the Royal household. Thus, in 1536, Henry VIII rented the ferry to John Pate who had been Keeper of the King's Wardrobe at Greenwich, while his daughter, Elizabeth I, granted ferry rights to one John Williams in consideration of his father's faithful service in the "Boyling House".

The ferrymen prospered when the Court moved by road and the Privy Purse accounts of the Tudor monarchs enumerated consider-able sums, varying from two shilling to six shillings and eightpence for ferry services at Richmond. Sometimes the ferrymen had the honour of rowing the Royal ladies, but usually the Sovereigns travelled up and down the river in their resplendent State barges, the glory of the Thames.

The poorest villagers fished strenuously for a living, casting their nets greedily into the Thames. In bygone centuries the fishing rights from West Shene to Petersham had belonged to the Carthusian monks, but after the Reformation the people were free to fish, although the Royal salmon was claimed by the Lord of the manor.

"This noble river, the Thames", wrote Harrison in Tudor times, "yieldeth not clots of gold as the Tagus doth, but an infinite plentie of excellent, sweet, and pleasante fish, wherewith such as inhabit neere unto her banks are fed and fullie nourished. What should I speake of the fat and sweet Salmons dailie taken in this streame, and that in such plentie after the time of the smelt be passed, as no river in Europa is able to exceed it. What store of Barbels, Trouts, Chenins, Pearches, Smelts, Breames, Roches, Daces, Gudgings, Flounders, Shrimps, etc., are commonlie to be had therein, I refer me to them that know by experience better than I, by reason of their dailie trade of fishing in the same. And albeit it seemeth from time to time, to be as it were defrauded in sundrie wise of these hir large commodities, by the insatiable avarice of the fishermen, yet this famous river complaineth commonlie of no want; but the more it looseth at one time, the more it yieldeth at another. Onelie in carps it seemeth to be scant, though it is not long since that kind of fish was brought to England . . . Oh, that this river might be spared but even one yeare from nets, etc! But alas then should manie a poor man be undone."

4

"*Sceone . . . syenes . . . schenes . . . schene . . . shene.*" Anglo-Saxon peasants uttered the words in their varied forms to express their admiration of the place with the silver river and the green hill and so the name Sheen developed into its modern form. It was not mentioned in the Domesday Book, for like Ham with Hatch (*Ham* in this district meant a dwelling with a water-meadow and *Hatch*, a gate), it lay within the demesne of Royal Kingston-upon-Thames and was Crown property. And, with the exception of two periods, from that time to this present day, Richmond has been a Royal manor, although the Sovereign has leased it frequently to a subject.

The land between Shene and Ham had its place in the Norman record for it was owned by Chertsey Abbey, in whose possession it remained until Henry V's reign. The Domesday Book surveyors called this manor *Patrichesam*, which in medieval times evolved into *Petersamwere*, and then became Petersham. At the time of the great reckoning it owned a church, arable land with fifteen villeins, three acres of meadow, a fishery of one thousand eels and as many lampreys.

Two facts emerge from the mists that dim Shene's history at the end of the Norman dynasty: a small church was built there, shortly after Gilbert, Sheriff of Surrey, founded Merton Abbey and endowed it with the advowson of Kingston-upon-Thames and a chain of local chapelries. The other event occurred when Henry I, who stayed in his manor house by the river at Shene in 1125, gave the manor to John Belet and its first period of subject-ownership began. The name of the Belet family was entered in the Roll of Battle Abbey, and the manor was a grant of serjeantry made, according to the feudal custom, in return for butler service. It was held for over a century by the Belet family and we catch a glimpse of Michael, a magnificent figure at the coronation of Henry II's consort, Queen Eleanor.

Shene was valued at sixteen pounds, eight shillings and eleven-pence-halfpenny when it was inherited by Michael's nieces, Emma and Alice. Emma's share included the manor-house, a dovecot, a park, a pasture, a rabbit-warren and a free fishery. She had sixteen acres of meadow and two hundred acres of arable land worth four-pence an acre, in addition to her tenants' rents and their customary labour. Alice's moiety was slightly less; her two hundred acres of arable land were valued at only twopence the acre, but she received additional meadowland, the pasture of an island in the Thames called the Winyard, and assurance of help from her tenants in harvest-time.

That was the picture Shene presented in mid-Plantagenet days, but the children of these first Ladies of the manor did not benefit from their mothers' inheritance. In 1264, Emma, who married

Jordan Oliver, restored her lands to Edward I in the Royal presence and then deeds inscribed with the word "Shene" exchanged hands once or twice, until they rested in the coffers of Brunel, Bishop of Bath and Wells, who owned Ham. (The Lord of Ham provided Kingston-upon-Thames with a clove of gilliflower—a clove weighed seven or eight pounds—twice yearly, and after King John's death, promised three cloves to that town for the next coronation.) Ham passed from Brunel's heirs to the Lovells of Minster Lovell, Oxfordshire, who held it until Henry VII forfeited these estates after the presumed death of Francis, "Lovell the Dog", at the Battle of Stoke-on-Trent.

When Brunel died Edward I acquired the Bishop's share of Shene. By that time the King held the other half of the manor for he had confiscated Alice Belet's inheritance—her son, John de Valletort had failed to pay some feudal fee. King Edward found his manor-house by the Thames attractive and he was in residence when the Scottish nobles came to treat with him after William Wallace's execution.

His son Edward II used this riverside home occasionally—documents relating to his reign were issued from Shene—and he ordered twenty-four Carmelite Friars to go to the Royal manor. They were granted a dwelling-place with three islands in the Thames and some enclosures, but their stay was brief, for two years later they were reported to have moved to the North Gate, Oxford.

The first mention of building operations at Shene occurred when Ralph Thurbane was ordered to take carpenters, tile-covers of houses and workmen to repair the Royal residence for the Lady of the manor, Edward II's widow, Queen Isabella of France, whom Froissart thought the most beautiful woman in the world. Her estate there was valued at thirty pounds a year, but it was a happy day for the village when she surrendered it with her other lands to her son in exchange for a pension, for a golden phase opened which sealed it as the home of kings.

Edward III adorned the manor-house with tapestries and *objets d'art* he had captured in the French wars. The glades of Shene rang with hunting-horns, the meadows with trumpets summoning the knights to jousts. In the vivid poetry of Geoffrey Chaucer, Yeoman of the King's Chamber, later a Squire of the Royal Household, we sense the joyful atmosphere of the gilded Court, of those enchanted days by the Thames. We walk with him early one morning as he encounters a "world of ladies": they wear white velvet surcoats studded with gems and chaplets of leaves adorn their hair.

The ladies laugh as they ride by and he wanders on, up the tracks of the green hill, where he hears the music of water trickling from springs, flowing in many directions. Then he goes to the hostel which, with chapel and cell, is maintained by Merton Abbey for travellers and listens to the talk of the pilgrims who have crossed Surrey. (This hostel stood close to the foot of the present Compass Hill, its site identified this century during examination of property deeds.)

Chaucer referred directly to the Royal manor in the Prologue to the *Legend of Good Women*:

> And whan this book is maad yive hit the queene
> On my behalfe at Eltham or at Shene.

This queen was Richard II's first wife, Anne of Bohemia, who found the riverside manor-house so charming in the summer that Richard beautified it to please her and Chaucer, as Clerk of the Works, may have played his part in its improvement. But these embellishments did not survive for, according to Stow, when Anne died in the Palace, the King, crazy with grief, ordered it to be destroyed. It is believed that his instructions were only partially carried out and that it decayed through neglect. Queen Anne, who rode round the Royal manor in a novel fashion—she introduced the side-saddle into England—may have influenced Richard to show consideration for his tenants at Shene; he exempted them from demands made upon them customarily by the officers of purveyance for corn and other provisions for the Palace larder.

Richard II's reign opened at Shene, for he was taken there on June 21st, 1377, as his old grandfather, Edward III, expired. The manor-house lay in shadow and the Royal favourite, Alice Perrers, had stolen away unobtrusively, laden with her spoil—silver dishes, bedclothing, silks and all the pretty things her acquisitive fingers could collect, even, according to tradition, the rings she removed

24

5   Richmond Hill: A Fête on the Prince Regent's Birthday

From the painting by J. M. W. Turner

6 "The Prospect of Richmo

From a print published

Surrey", about 1726

nry Overton and J. Hook

7 Richmond Hill: The Terrace and Meadows

from the dying monarch's fingers. The very next day a group of noblemen assembled before the boy king in one of the colourful State apartments, and solemnly handed him the Great Seal of England in a white leather purse, which Uncle John, Duke of Lancaster, took from him immediately and gave to Nicholas Bonde, Knight of the King's Chamber, to keep safely.

Twenty-two years later Richard's reign ended at Shene, where he was conducted, a broken, degraded captive, and Froissart chronicled: "Thus the Duke of Lancaster departed from Chertsey and rode to Shene and from thence in the night they conveyed the King to the Tower of London . . ."

5

The story of the Royal manor from 1414 through many decades is one of incessant building activities, for Henry V's architectural ideas were of a grandiose character. He ordered Richard's neglected home to be rebuilt as a castle—in the first years of his reign, Henry VII frequently headed documents "Our Castle at Shene". He founded the Carthusian monastery, the House of Jesus of Bethlehem, near the river in the Royal Park in West Shene (today we know this as the Old Deer Park), and the Monastery of St. Bridget of Syon was erected on the opposite bank. It was removed a few years later to the present site of Syon House.

John du Pont restocked the Palace gardens where Chaucer's "world of ladies" had walked, and planted trees and herbs: John Straunge, Clerk of the Works, received fifty-two shillings, laid out by him as payment to the carver, Robert Broune, for "carving divers swans in the King's Chamber at Shene".

Warrants poured out to purveyors to find materials, to impress labourers for the works in the Royal manor: directions reached Yorkshire for certain men to "take carriage" for stone ordered by Straunge for Shene: the county of Kent was searched for labourers and requisites. Fleets of barges came up the Thames, laden with stone, iron, lime, timber, and later with glass, and unloaded at a wharf near the monastery. The latter, the largest Charterhouse in England, took years to build and the date of its completion was unrecorded. It was 1,725 feet long, over 1,300 feet broad, and its water was obtained from springs, drawn through subterranean conduits. Its site was indicated as "running from Hokelot by Diversbusshe on the south to Armetteslote on the north".

The works at Shene went on long after Henry V had ended his life in France, and, anxious to speed them up, in 1437, young Henry VI ordered the brickmaker, William Vesey, to find land suitable for the tiles that were known as bricks. Some thirty years later "Le Breikhouse of West Shene" was referred to as a boundary to additional acres given to the monks by Edward IV's consort, Elizabeth Woodville, then Lady of the Royal manor.

A copy of an interesting document, dating from Edward IV's reign, was kept in the late Lord Dysart's famous library at Ham House. It comprised a set of regulations called "Rules of Customes", laid down for the tenants of Shene, Petersham and Ham, and related chiefly to leases, pasture rights, timber for repairs and furze for firewood. The most important clause stipulated that copyhold property should be inherited by the youngest son, or failing a youngest son, by the youngest daughter. For centuries these rules guided the procedure at each Court Baron, the meeting at which the Lord of the manor or his steward and the tenants discussed the land granted to the latter by "the King and Kings Time out of Mind".

Chapter II

SIXTEENTH-CENTURY SCENE

Henry VII's Palace—Lancaster Herald—Princess Margaret's Wedding—
Legend of Hidden Gold—Henry VIII's Magnificence—New Fashions in
Masques—Wolsey—Anne of Cleves

I

A T the end of the fifteenth century, the Palace at "Kynge's Shene", as the Royal manor was described in a contemporary document, was delivered once again into craftsmen's hands. They had instructions to rebuild it quickly, for the Privy Lodgings had been destroyed by a fire which broke out in the evening of December 21st, 1497. King Henry VII and his family, prepared to celebrate Christmas, were conducted to a safe place, but flames, crackling until midnight, destroyed furniture, tapestries and decorations. When the fire had been extinguished, the ashes were searched for treasures and the Privy Purse accounted for twenty pounds, "for rewardes yeven to them that founde the King's juels at Shene".

The Queen, Elizabeth of York, wept at the loss of the Palace. She and her sisters had been reared at Shene, when it reflected the brilliancy of her father's Court, and she had known the manor-house in the grey days that had followed his death.

Henry VII was enchanted with the Royal manor directly he saw it and it became his favourite home. Modern research has proved that Henry did not ill-treat his mother-in-law, but doubtless he was relieved when she retreated to a Bermondsey convent and left the Palace to the lusty young House of Tudor.

Elizabeth of York dried her tears when she heard that her husband had decided to rebuild the Palace on a magnificent scale. The disaster gave Henry an opportunity to express his aesthetic inclinations, so often submerged in the astute statesman, to indulge in dreams, dreams that were realised in sweeping stone vistas, in tall columns and fan-vaulting as refined as lacework. He intended to adorn Shene with a residence that would be an elaborate frame for sovereignty, would impress foreign statesmen with the power of the Tudors.

An item in the Privy Purse accounts, dated 1505, proves that the master mason, Henry Smyth, was associated with the work—"Delivered to Henry Smyth for fynissyng of the towre at Richemont and paving both galoryes and ledying of the said towre and paying for bryke and stone and other diverse works, as appereth by a bill signed £133 6s 9d." Thomas Mauncy, former Warden of the Carpenters' Company, held the office of King's Carpenter while the building was in progress. A petition sent to Wolsey in 1521 revealed that Henry VII had employed foreign joiners in the reconstruction of the Palace at Richmond: fashionable Italian decorators were commissioned to embellish the State apartments.

The third Royal home of Shene occupied its former site, an area of ten acres, extending from the Thames to the Green. The new building was colourful and stimulating, with its recognition of the Gothic tradition and its hint of the coming Renaissance, its clustered octagonal vanes, gilded crockets, pinnacles and vanes.

King Henry, riding round his manor in green doublet and ermine-bordered purple velvet mantle, was proud of his achievement. He remembered his youth as the Earl of Richmond, his title taken from that town in Yorkshire, named first by the Breton, Earl Alan, whose castle stood on its fertile hill. And as he looked from the windows of his Thames Valley home, Henry saw another green promontory and he directed that henceforth the place should be known officially as Richmond. But part of the Royal manor retained its ancient name and documents described it as "Richemont *alias* West Shene".

The Archway above the main entrance to Richmond Palace was finished with a stone plaque, on which were sculptured Henry VII's arms and supporters. They were unlike those borne by any other English Monarch: the shield was held on one side by the Red Dragon of the House of Cadwalader, from which Henry claimed descent, while the other supporter was the Greyhound of York, replaced by Henry VIII by the Lion of England.

As we look today at the Red Dragon and the Greyhound, now approximately four and a half centuries old, their outlines are indefinite and shadowy, for time has attenuated them. The four-centred

Perpendicular arch, 18 feet high, 11 feet 3 inches wide, has been much restored, sometimes with Tudor bricks removed from an unwanted wall on the site. Stapled to its sides are four rusty iron gatepins which held the vanished oak gate, guarded by the sentry who stood in the recess beneath the smaller arch.

2

He who seeks to visualise the Palace as it was when its re-edifying was almost finished, finds a guide in the description of Lancaster Herald, whose manuscript is in the College of Arms. Lancaster Herald accompanied the Royal party when Henry VII took his new daughter-in-law, Catherine of Aragon, and her Spanish entourage, to spend a gay week-end in his country home. A few days previously the Princess had been married to Arthur, Prince of Wales, who died six months later.

The Herald related how that November evening in 1501, the party disembarked from barges in the neighbouring village of Mortlake—an indication that the water-gate at Richmond was un-finished at that date—and, the way illuminated by torches, rode to the Palace, which he described as "this ertheley and secunde Paradise". He observed that the building was quadrangular and foursquare, encompassed by an unusual brick wall, studded with towers, its strong oak gates, "stikkyd full of nailys right thikke, and crossed wt barres of iron".

He noticed the abundant windows in the galleries and paused in the second, smaller court beyond the Middle Gate, to admire the pure water as it ran from a stone conduit or cistern. Its upper part—the fountain—was decorated with lions, red dragons and branches of red roses. The water came from the streams trickling down the slopes of the Royal manor, directed into conduits through leaden pipes and thence to another conduit near the Palace. One supply came from the White Conduit at the Hill summit, another flowed through the Red Conduit (which was situated in what today is Paradise Road), while a third was placed beyond the ferry at the entrance to the present Petersham Road, and ran down into the "kynge's strete", near the Palace. Evidence of this costly water supply has come to light from time to time and in 1909 when workmen widened a road, they cut into the Red Conduit and revealed a 4-foot chamber containing clear water. It was protected by a Tudor arch, its lower part, half stone, half brick. The floor was laid with chalk slabs and a massive stone doorway formed the entrance to the reservoir or receiving-chamber.

The Herald went into the Great Hall at the right of the Middle Court. It was paved with tiles and its novel timber roof pleased him—it was neither beamed nor braced and was decorated with carved knots and hanging pendants. Between the "wyndowes glassid right lightsume and goodly", were portraits of English kings, and holding falchions and swords, they resembled "bold and valiaunt knights". He saw a tapestry woven with classical battle scenes and indeed, "the hole apparement wos most glorious and joyefull to consider and beholde". This Great Hall, 100 feet long, 40 feet wide, had a screen at one end and a minstrel's gallery. The hearth for the fire was in the centre of the floor and the smoke was emitted through the domed turret called the louvre, its exterior elaborately fretted and coloured.

He went to the other side of the Middle Court and climbed steps to the Chapel Royal, which, 96 feet long, and 30 feet broad, was on the second storey, its undercroft used as a wine cellar. The Chapel Royal was glorious with arras, cloth of gold and jewels and its walls adorned with pictures of saints.

The Royal Collection at Windsor includes a Votive Painting of St. George and the Dragon, which Horace Walpole who owned it, believed was commissioned by Henry VII for the Richmond Palace Chapel. It was executed by a Flemish artist in oil colours upon oak panels, is 4 feet 8 inches high and is almost square. It depicts Henry, Elizabeth of York and their sons and daughters and they kneel, as the Dragon transfixed with a broken tilting spear, flies across the sky towards St. George, waiting to smite with his sword. A castle and a building like a temple, which has a ball and steeple, are painted into the landscape, and the Tudor emblems, the portcullis and the rose are blazoned. The painting was acquired by Queen Victoria when the notable Strawberry Hill collection was sold.

From the Chapel Royal, the Herald visited the King's Privy Closet which was hung with silks, furnished with a carpet and cushions. A curtain closed off Henry's private chapel, where the altar gleamed with golden relics and precious stones. The ceiling was decorated with azure timber lozenges, like checks, each check enclosing a gilt-tipped rose or portcullis. Round the Chapel Royal were other apartments used by the Queen and her children and by "my Lady the Kyng's mother", Margaret Beaufort, Countess of Richmond. Beneath the windows of the Royal apartments he saw pleasant gardens, ornamented with carved lions and dragons and the paths led to bowling-alleys, archery butts and summer-houses for chess and card playing. And as he looked up, wherever his eyes travelled, they glimpsed weather-vanes fashioned with the King's arms, painted in rich gold and azure, so that "the heryng in a wyndy day was right marvellous to knowe and undrestond".

Henry VII established a library at Richmond Palace and bought many rare books, especially French ones. These were placed in the care of Quintin Poulet (sometimes spelt "Paulet"), a Fleming from Lille, who copied manuscripts for the King. One of these, executed in 1496, a moral treatise entitled *L'Imaginacyon de vraye Noblesse*, which can be seen in the British Museum, is a delightful relic of the Tudor dynasty at Shene. Each page is illuminated with a wide, pale gold border, adorned with delicately painted flowers and its coloured plates glow with sapphire, amber, ruby and emerald. One depicts Henry, in a rich blue mantle, bending forward to receive the book from the librarian.

3

In January 1503, trumpeters went to the leads of a turret of Richmond Palace and played a silvery fanfare across the Thames, grey in its winter dress, and the villagers knew that the King's eldest daughter, thirteen-year-old Princess Margaret, had been married in the Palace to James IV of Scotland, the Earl of Bothwell acting as proxy-bridegroom. Elizabeth of York, expecting a baby, was unwell and a "quiet" Royal wedding had been arranged at Richmond, celebrated however, by a round of entertainments for the visiting Scotsmen—banquets, pageants and jousts on the Green.

Suddenly all were stopped and tears replaced mirth for news came that the Queen, who had gone to the Tower of London for her confinement, was dead.

During the following months, the Royal widower issued many orders from Richmond for Queen Margaret of Scotland's trousseau —furnishings, dresses, shoes and hose, and in the summer, when she left her home, riding a white palfrey, he accompanied his daughter on the first stage of her journey.

Henry VII survived his wife six years, and a sick man, he signed his will at Richmond at the end of March 1509. He desired that his executors should spend two thousand pounds upon the repair of highways and bridges from Windsor to Richmond, which in our Royal manor resulted in the improvement of a street—probably the road from London, the Great or Common Street. Then, as the gardens Lancaster Herald had admired, donned April dress, he died. Despite his directions that the obsequies should be simple, his body was borne with full panoply from his Privy Closet to the Chapel Royal before it was taken by road to the superb resting-place he had prepared in Westminster Abbey. Three hundred and thirty poor men each earned four shillings for carrying torches in the funeral procession.

He left nearly two million pounds and after his death, rumours spread that he had concealed money in Richmond Palace to safe-guard it from his extravagant, grasping son. The tale lingered through the centuries and there was an echo in 1936 when a metal-diviner, misinformed about facts, wrote to King Edward VIII and asked permission to search for the hidden gold in "Richmond Castle". Early this century when cellars in the Old Palace were being repaired, strange, unaccountable cavities, like long, narrow pockets were found in the walls and local archaeologists suggested that they may have been constructed as safes for Henry's money.

Not a coin came to light and it is probable that Henry VIII dis-covered his father's fortune and spent it—but he maintained his pre-decessor's belief that monarchy should be framed sumptuously. The Venetian envoys who went to Richmond one St. George's Day—Henry VIII sometimes held the Investiture of the Order of the Garter in this Chapel Royal—were dazzled by the King of

England's opulence. Their eyes opened at the halberdiers in silver breast-plates stationed in the galleries: " . . . and by God, they were all as big as giants so that the display was very grand", wrote Pietro Pasqualigo to his friends in Venice. The King leaned against a gold brocade cushion on a chair upholstered in the same material and the canopy over his head was heavily embroidered with gold. His violet robe shimmered over a doublet, striped, Swiss fashion, in white and crimson, his slashed hose was scarlet, his crimson velvet cap elaborately worked.

But it was a round-cut diamond suspended from his gold collar which awed the Venetians—Pasqualigo compared its size to that of a walnut. He noticed the massive gold dishes with covers which appeared at the banquet and the tapestries on the walls. Henry VIII's passion for collecting tapestries had begun and the inventory of these, taken after his death, included many pieces in Richmond Palace. They depicted classical and Biblical scenes such as "Kinge Salamon giving judgmente to two women of their children", and "Nabugodonoser" which, still there in the mid-seventeenth century, was sold by Oliver Cromwell's agent for three pounds. There were "Verdours with fountaines and beastes" and "windowe pieces of tapestry", ten of them with bells in "thupper borders".

The Venetian ambassador's secretary, Nicola Sagudino, thought the voices of the Chapel choristers were "rather divine than human—they did not chant but sang like angels. . . ." The musician, William Cornyshe, was responsible at one period for the singing of the Chapel Royal children. He composed one of Henry VIII's favourite songs, "Blow Thy Horn, Hunter", and devised Court masques.

A new note was introduced into these revels at Richmond "after the manner of Italy", and instead of hired performers, the courtiers and sometimes the King himself, presented the entertainments. The accounts of Richard Gibson, in charge of costumes, indicate extensive preparations for one such masque. Many yards of white, crimson, green and yellow satin were used to dress twenty-eight lords and ladies and six minstrels: garments were unearthed from the King's old store of "Bregys" satin and decorated with copper spangles: "Almain" doublets of blue and crimson velvet, lined with cloth of gold, scintillated with jewels borrowed from the Royal treasures.

Harry Gyllforth arranged an entertainment in the Great Hall on Epiphany night in 1511 and the showpiece was a golden stock tree, its branches adorned with roses and pomegranates. It stood on a hill out of which came a merry troop of Morris dancers. The stage properties included over 1000 bells for the dancers, 29,000 spangles, gold foil, silver paper and 600 white "whickers" to entwine in the tree. But of that night it was reported, "The Queen's Grace in her chamber of a prince whose soul is among the holy innocents."

Henry participated in a joust on Richmond Green on April 19th, 1515, and wore a coat, which, with saddle covering and trappings for his horse, required twenty/nine yards of blue velvet at thirteen shillings the yard and an abundance of white satin. A quarter of this garment was borne into the field and lost, the "residue . . . past the King's wearing by a shower of rain".

4

Henry VIII appropriated Cardinal Wolsey's new country home, Hampton Court, a few miles up the river, and the Cardinal was invited, in return, to use Richmond Palace as a residence. In 1525 he celebrated Christmas there with such a display of ostentation that his critics carped: "Soe a butcher's dogge doth lie in the mannor of Richmond."

Wolsey returned to the Royal manor after he had passed the climax of his career, and disaster approached. This time he moved into the modest lodge in West Shene, built by Dean Colet, who had hoped to end his own life there in pious retirement. It was situated close to the Carthusian monastery (in the acres we know today as the Old Deer Park) and until he set out for his last fateful journey to his diocese of York, the Cardinal constantly sought the company of the senior monks, with whom he discussed the follies of the vain/ glorious world.

But the days of the monks were numbered, and in 1539 the House of Jesus of Bethlehem was suppressed; the Prior was pensioned and the monks given money to enable them to travel to the Continent. They left an unusual object in one of their lumber/rooms—a corpse, believed to be that of Henry VIII's late brother/in/law, James IV of

38

Scotland, slain at the Battle of Flodden Field in 1513. The English victors encased it in lead and had taken it to Henry. He had refused it decent burial and it had been deposited in the monastery.

Stow related the sequel in his Elizabethan *Survey of London*: ". . . I have been shown the same body so lapped in lead, close to the head and body, thrown into a waste room amongst the old timber, lead, and other rubble. Since the which time workmen there, for their foolish pleasure, hewed off his head; and Launcelot Young, master glazier to her majesty, feeling a sweet savour to come from thence, and seeing the same dried from all moisture, and yet the form re-maining, with the hair of the head, and beard red, brought it to London to his house in Wood Street, where for a time he kept it for the sweetness, but in the end caused the sexton of that church to bury it amongst other bones taken out of their charnel, etc."

The unhappy, eclipsed Princess Mary was ordered sometimes to stay at Richmond Palace with her half-sister, the baby Elizabeth, and a report sent by the Spanish ambassador, Chapuys, to his master, the Emperor Charles V, in 1534, tells its own story of the domestic life of the Tudors at this period. He wrote how, when the King's daughters were at Richmond, "there came the Lady Anne, herself, accompanied by the dukes of Norfolk and Suffolk and others and by a party of ladies on the pretence of visiting her daughter, but in reality to see and salute the Princess—a great novelty, no doubt. The Princess, however, would not leave her room until the Lady had actually taken her departure from the house that she might not see her." So the tactless Anne Boleyn rode back to Hampton Court, while Mary, whose health at the time was delicate, consoled herself with her music and her Spanish friends.

Henry VIII was seen frequently at Richmond Palace in later life, but then he went as a guest, entertained by his fourth and divorced wife, Anne of Cleves, on whom, with other lands, he settled the Royal manor. They supped so merrily that presently it was rumoured that Anne had given birth to a "fair boy", of whom Henry was the father. The perplexed Sovereign, then the doting husband of Catherine Howard, caused an official inquiry to be made and the rumour was traced to an indiscreet needlewoman who had been employed in the Palace.

Anne of Cleves lived tranquilly at Richmond, interested in her gardens, her dresses and in the Princess Elizabeth who was allowed to stay with her stepmother. After Henry VIII's death, she was obliged to surrender the Palace to the boy king, Edward VI, an unnecessary demand for the lad seldom stayed there. He was at Richmond, however, for a few days when the Duke of North-umberland's son, Robert Dudley, married Amy Robsart at West Shene, and he was the guest of honour at their wedding.

The poor people of the Royal manor were remembered by Anne of Cleves when she made her will, and she left them four pounds, to be given to them by the churchwardens.

Chapter III

ELIZABETHAN ERA

*Thomas Platter—"Red Lyon" and "Golden Hynde"—Parish Registers—An
Evening in the Palace—Dr. Dee—Fashionable Kew—Spanish Armada—
Shakespeare—Death of Elizabeth I*

I

ONE Sunday in October 1599, a German traveller, Thomas Platter, and his friends hired a coach to take them from London to Richmond. Like many foreigners who came to England at the end of the iridescent Elizabethan age, they obtained passes into the Royal residences. They reached the Palace just in time to see Elizabeth I walk from the Presence Chamber to the Chapel Royal, and as she passed along the gallery, she noticed that some of her subjects knelt below in the Courtyard, waiting to see her. She put her head out of the window and cried, "God bless my people"—to Platter it sounded like "piple", and they all responded, "God save the Queen." They remained on their knees until she made a sign and he was deeply impressed by the reverence they expressed when they rose to their feet.

Platter and his friends lingered while the Queen listened to a short sermon, and saw her return to the Presence Chamber. They had inspected Royal treasures elsewhere and they spent the remainder of their time at the Palace playing tennis. Then, refusing offers of hospitality, for they feared they would be detained, they went to a local inn for a repast before they returned to London.

There were two flourishing hostelries near the Palace at this period —the "Golden Hynde" and the "Red Lyon". The "Golden Hynde", which changed its name in the next reign to the "Feathers" in honour of Henry, Prince of Wales, stood by the Town Lane (later Water Lane). It functioned for about two hundred years and then, rebuilt, was occupied as offices until 1908 and during its demolition, its original gable ends and a half-timbered wall were exposed.

The "Red Lyon" opened in 1520 and at the time Platter went to

Richmond, one Merriall was the innkeeper. It had its own fields and orchards and its commodious premises faced Great Street, while its courtyard extended to the site known today as Red Lion Street. Travellers from London turned to the left where the road from Clapham bifurcated and as they approached it, they passed the Church and the Red Conduit. The "Red Lyon" had a long life, although it experienced many vicissitudes and now and then the Court Rolls of the manor referred to it as "the late Red Lyon". It always reopened and it was not until 1909 that the last public-house which bore the ancient name, vanished from Richmond. But that was not the well-equipped building of Tudor times, although it retained the site; the licence had been transferred and there only remained a small, squalid dwelling, surrounded by slums.

The road from Clapham passed a boundary of the Royal manor known as Marsh Gate, where the ground was so boggy that even at a later date, cattle foundered in it. At the end of the Elizabethan era, Richmond was studded with stiles and gates and Marsh Gate was alluded to sometimes as Pentecost Gate, doubtless after the local family whose name was entered into the Parish Registers.

The faded handwriting, brown with age, in these long, narrow volumes which date from 1583, gives us a clue to some of the ordinary people who lived in Richmond during Elizabeth I's reign—the Lovells, the Standons, the Gisbyes, the Cogdells or Cockdells, and the Tyes or Ties, who were butchers. The Court Leet records of Kingston-upon-Thames remind us how often they filled the customary manorial offices as constables, tithing-men, aleconners and headboroughs. One of the Tyes, who lived in Brewers Lane, was associated with the Martin Marprelate plot—the country was flooded with pamphlets which accused the clergy of neglecting their duties. Tye hid papers in his house for one of the suspected authors, John Udall of Kingston-upon-Thames.

The deaths of some of the Queen's servants were recorded in the Parish Registers, such as that of Edward Spencer, Yeoman of the Scullery, Rob'te Euans, Yeoman of the Guard, and John Terry of the Buttery, whose decease was set down without date or month in a list which included a poor unknown described as "One of the Stable at Shenne". A sensational tragedy occurred at the Palace in November 1599, when the Register stated that Mistress Elizabeth Ratcliff, a Maid of Honour had died and her bowels had been buried in the chancel of the Parish Church. She had pined away after the death of her brother, Sir Alexander, and it was reported that when she expired, the Queen commanded that her body should be opened; it was stated to be well and sound, except for certain strings striped all over her heart.

In the dark months before Queen Mary died in 1558, Richmond Palace had been quiescent. Then with Elizabeth I's accession it crashed into the final brilliant movement of the Tudor symphony, its State rooms thronged with the influential and the ambitious. Once the sombre figure of Father Chauncy, the Carthusian Prior, wended its way among the prismatic raiment of the young courtiers. He had decided to plead with the Queen, to beg her to allow the monks to remain in West Shene, but a friend who saw him before he approached her, realising the futility of his errand, led him gently away. The monks left the House of Jesus of Bethlehem for the second and last time in 1559 and presently reports reached them that the spirits of their dead brethren, buried within its precincts, haunted their old home and could be heard chanting at night.

2

Edmund Bohun, one of Elizabeth I's earliest biographers, described how she spent her days at Richmond. The morning's official business over, she walked in the galleries or in the garden. Then, he stated, she took her coach and passed in the sight of her people to the neighbouring groves and fields and sometimes hunted or hawked. But she was not always in the pumpkin-shaped vehicle for she often rode horseback, her Master of the Horse, Sir Robert Dudley, later Lord Leicester, at her side. Did the local housewives —the Gisbyes, the Cockdells, the Lovells and the rest—peer through their lattice-windows as the twain passed and shake their heads knowingly, especially when gossip reached them concerning a possible Royal wedding? First, there was talk of the King of Sweden as bridegroom and for his entertainment at Richmond, the Queen commanded the Duke of Norfolk to lay in an appropriate stock of wine and beer. Some years later came the Duc d'Anjou, who was accommodated in a house near the Palace.

The Queen had a chequer-rail placed outside the Palace to protect its walls—possibly that was after the French ambassador, invited to hunt in the Royal Park, chased three stags on to the Green and killed them "before her gate". The villagers were free to approach the rail and climb a stile at the end of it. But for a description of a scene within we rely on a report sent in July 1564, by Guzman da Silva to his master, King Philip II of Spain. Elizabeth received him in the garden and, "We then went into a very large gallery where she took me aside for nearly an hour . . ." (The long gallery was a useful promenade where conversations could not be overheard.) Supper was served with customary ceremony and he was about to take his leave when the Queen invited him to see a comedy, produced in the Great Hall which was illuminated by torchlight. A masque followed, presented by courtiers in black and white, Elizabeth's colours, and one handed her a sonnet of praise.

After that "The Queen entered a gallery where there was a very long table with every sort and kind of preserves and candied fruits that can be imagined, according to the English custom. It must have been two in the morning and the Queen had to return to Westminster by water, although it was very windy." Elizabeth's State Barge was rowed by twenty-five watermen and, elaborately carved, its cabin windows were a novel feature.

Another visitor to Richmond told how the Queen "inclined her ear unto my simple song". He was Edmund Spenser, taken into the Royal presence by Sir Walter Raleigh, and he carried with him a section of *The Faerie Queen*, which she permitted him to read to her. The poem appeared in 1590, with a flourishing dedication to Elizabeth I, who conferred on the author an annual pension of fifty pounds.

3

Sometimes when the Queen rode to "take ayre", she cantered across the fields to Mortlake to call on Dr. John Dee, who lived in a rambling old house, west of the church. Dee was an astrologer, alchemist, mathematician, cartographer and, in the opinion of his neighbours—a wizard. She arrived at his house one afternoon in March 1574, at an awkward time for Dee had just buried his first wife in the churchyard across the road. Hearing this, Elizabeth refused to enter, but she teased the widower to bring out a certain mirror that she wished to see. She dismounted and stood by the wall of the church her father had built, while he explained the properties of the novel glass.

Dee, adviser to overseas explorers, was consulted by the leading navigators—the Gilberts, Hawkins and Frobisher: he plotted maps for them and discussed routes for expeditions which founded the British Commonwealth. These visitors often came up the river from London and traces of the watergate at the end of Dee's garden are still perceptible from the Mortlake towing-path. His rewards from the Queen for his varied services were meagre, but sometimes she sent money when she wished him to entertain illustrious foreigners. These visitors manifested a deep interest in his belief that he could realise the alchemist's age-long dream and discover how to transmute base metals into gold. (His research was stimulated by the *séances* he held with his medium, Kelly, and he sought advice from the most distinguished archangels). At last one of these illustrious foreigners, Albertus Alasco, Free Baron of Lasco, Palatine of Saradia, Poland, persuaded Dee to accompany him when he returned to the Continent. As soon as the alchemist and his family had left Mortlake, a mob broke into his house, destroyed priceless books, smashed rare scientific instruments. Dee did not return for fifteen years, and when he came back to England, his dreams of making limitless gold unfulfilled, the Elizabethan age was nearly over.

Mortlake High Street is drab today with meandering brewery yards and small, old-fashioned shops leading to the church . . . yet, as we stand there, time's hour-glass tilts back, the grey atmosphere is transformed into cornfields and a man with a long milk-white beard bows low to a red-headed queen, who has paid him a signal honour, for she has drawn off one of her elegant gloves and given him her hand to kiss.

Dee recorded facts about the neighbourhood in his fat, sheepskin-bound diaries . . . in October 1580, for example, there was a heavy

45

storm and six people were drowned in the Kew ferry-boat. This hamlet, where the herbalist, Dr. William Turner, had found the soil admirable for his horticultural experiments, had grown fashion-able since Elizabeth's aunt, Princess Mary, widow of Louis XII of France, had lived there with her second husband, the Duke of Suffolk. Lord Leicester owned the Dairie House and fished at the end of the grounds, a soothing relaxation from the high-pitched tempo of the Court. It is believed that he and Amy Robsart spent their honeymoon there and that when news reached the Court of her mysterious death, the Queen ordered him to remain in retreat at Kew for a few days.

In 1595 she visited the hamlet and dined with Sir John Puckering, an honour he had long sought. It was an expensive entertainment for as she arrived, he presented her with a diamond-handled fan and a bouquet in which jewels mingled with flowers. When she retired to her privy chamber after a long and costly banquet, he gave her a "faire paire of virginals", and she found a "gown juppin" awaiting her in the bedroom. To express her pleasure at her reception, she took, uninvited from Sir John, a salt, a spoon and an agate fork.

There is the mighty trunk of an ancient, decrepit elm on Queen Elizabeth's Lawn, the riverside walk outside Kew Gardens, close to Kew Bridge. Its top branches have gone, its base has been treated with cement and, surrounded by recently planted youngsters, it is like Methuselah in a nursery-school. The local people call it "Queen Elizabeth's Tree", for she is believed to have been associ-ated with it—to have planted it or to have sat beneath its boughs. At the risk of tarnishing the arboreal legend, it must be stated that a Kew Gardens expert shakes his head when its age is mentioned. In his opinion the Venerable One was not touched by the Queen's long, white fingers and its leaves did not shade her burnished hair, but it is probably a shoot from the elm which flourished in the Elizabethan age.

4

The most dramatic scenes in Richmond's history occurred in the last days of July 1588. Elizabeth I sat in the Palace Council Chamber with her Ministers, drawing up plans for the defence of the realm as the Spanish Armada approached, and urgent documents were signed, orders concerning men and munitions. Inside the Palace the atmosphere was tense, laughter was arrested, rebecs and viols were silent.

The music was heard again the following year and the Queen, at Richmond, was reported to be in excellent spirits, dancing at least six or seven galliards every morning, strenuous exercise for a middle/aged woman.

One by one, the great figures of the age vanished and in 1598 William Cecil, Lord Burghley, died. He had owned a house at Richmond and for many years had been always on the spot, to advise and to pace the long gallery with Elizabeth. One Sunday morning there was a scene in the Palace, when Anthony Rudd, Bishop of St. David's, reminded her of the march of time by referring to the Royal wrinkles and grey hairs. The Queen opened a window and shouted that he should have kept his arithmetic to himself, and the Bishop was ordered to stay in his house as a punishment.

But time had compensated her with her people's deep esteem. A Richmond resident, Sir George Wright, founded local almshouses which have always borne her name. They overlooked the river, just beyond the ferry, until 1767, and by then they were in a derelict condition. They were rebuilt in the Vineyard and Queen Eliza/beth's Almshouses still provide homes for poor old women.

The weather was unusually severe in January 1603, and the Queen, unwell and dispirited, moved early that month from Whitehall to Richmond Palace, which she always termed her "warm winter/box". Her health improved. She dressed with her usual elegance and received a Venetian envoy. The Lord Chamber/lain sent for Shakespeare and his company to entertain her—Shake/speare had acted in his own plays many times before the Queen at Richmond—and they arrived on February 2nd, a memorable date, since it was the last occasion that Elizabeth I heard the magical phrases of the playwright whose name would crown her reign with undying lustre.

There is an old local tradition that when Shakespeare was in Richmond, he lodged with his friends, the Bardolphs, who lived at the end of a lane between Great Street and the Green. The legend has pinned itself to No. 1, the Green, doubtless because this interesting house, dormers in its high-pitched gables, is one of the oldest in the neighbourhood. But the story balances precariously on the fact that there is a white semicircular marble monument in the Parish Church erected to Simon Bardolph (who died in 1654) and his family. Research has failed to reveal the house, or even the site of the house the Bardolphs occupied.

Every town has its legends, those fascinating stories that colour a neighbourhood but defy proof. In Richmond the tale has echoed down the centuries that on March 24th, 1603, Elizabeth I died in the narrow apartment over the Old Palace Archway, then a mere passage between rooms. It is unsupported by historical evidence, it is highly improbable, and yet it is worth examination.

Contemporary accounts of the Queen's last days are conflicting: Sir Robert Carey, who saw her on the Saturday before she died, stated how she "gave command that the great closet should be prepared for her to go to chapel the next morning". But on the Sunday she was not seen and "one of the grooms came out, and bade make ready for the private closet; she would not go to the great. There we stayed long for her coming: but at last she had cushions laid for her in the privy chamber, hard by the closet door; and there she heard service. From that day forwards she grew worse and worse. She remained upon her cushions four days and nights, at the least." Carey is stated to have received a ring, dropped by his sister, Lady Scrope, from the window of the apartment over the Archway: this was a prearranged signal to tell him that the Queen was dead and that he could ride to Scotland and be the first to carry the news to James VI. In his *Memoirs* (written before 1627), he described how James knew his information was true as soon as he saw the ring.

Lady Southwell, who was in the Palace, reported that on one occasion the dying Queen stood upon her feet for fifteen hours. Elizabeth's mind wandered: probably she confused the past with the ungracious present and thought of her dead favourite, Essex, and a ring she had given him, a trinket which symbolised his submission and her forgiveness. Essex and the ring—two points of light flickering across her dark mind. It is at least plausible that, making a

48

final imperious gesture, she tottered down the long galley and so to the Gatehouse. To wait for the messenger, whom she thought would dash up with Essex's ring—the engraved blue-rimmed cameo that rests on her tomb in Westminster Abbey. Then she would be able to countermand the order for his execution and he would be restored to her.

Carey stated that the Lord Admiral was sent for and "What by fair means, what by force, he gat her to bed." The Gatehouse at Hampton Court was well furnished at this period and this may have been the case at Richmond, or they may have carried the Queen back to the Privy Lodgings before the curtain fell on the Tudor dynasty. The hypothesis cannot be ignored that if Elizabeth I did not actually expire in the Gatehouse, she lay there for some hours before her death, a fact known to the local people, hence the reason why this tale has been repeated through the centuries.

Panelled in pine, the Queen's Room extends as far as the sentry recess by the Archway. On the second floor of Gate House, as it is known nowadays, it is reached by a spiral stairway which twists up a turret. So little remains of Lancaster Herald's "secunde Paradise", of the Palace with the bright, fluttering vanes that Wyngaerde saw, of Elizabeth's "warm winter-box", which had had its most brilliant days when her body was borne down the Thames to Westminster. But despite alterations and adaptations, of periods of neglect, then over-zealous restoration, the three houses which comprise the remnant are charged with the Royal Tudor spirit, clean-cut and dominant, with the atmosphere of days when the sharp-edged axe was never far from gilded splendour.

On the left of Old Palace Yard, once part of the Great Court, is the long Wardrobe, restored in the late seventeenth or early eighteenth century, so that its steep tiled roof, finished with stone ball ornaments, is an acute contrast with the crenellated turret of Gate House, to which it is joined by small, uneven, old, wine-coloured bricks.

The other two dwellings are Gate House and the Old Palace (2, 3). Until 1939 the former formed a section of the Old Palace, but then the Crown, keeping abreast with modern times, partitioned walls in tortuous passages and converted the thirty odd rooms into two houses. Their façade, overlooking the Green is relieved by large semi-octagonal bays, each with castellated parapets and mullioned windows recessed in deep stone surrounds.

The fabric of Gate House shows original brickwork with faint, black, diamond-shaped checks, while near the parapet, black glazed Royal Tudor arrows point downward. The Old Palace has a fine Jacobean staircase. On the first floor is the narrow passage in which, during the eighteen-eighties, two Elizabethan dresses were found in a chest. Richmond's oldest residents know the facts and the discovery was mentioned in contemporary newspapers. This passage has been built in front of a Tudor window and its perpendicular stone surround has impressed its lines like a silhouette against a snow-white partition wall, uncanny relic of bygone centuries.

Chapter IV

EARLY SEVENTEENTH-CENTURY YEARS

Court Rolls of Royal Manor—Henry, Prince of Wales—John Hutchinson's Romance—Vinkeboons and Hollar—The New Park—The Plague

I

BY 1603 Richmond had been divided into Upper and Lower Fields and then partitioned into shotts—a "shott" being the Anglo-Saxon definition of a parcel of land. Such divisions as the Maybush, the Upper and Lower Dunstables, the East and West Bancrofts, all in the Upper Field, have vanished from local topography, but Parkshot is a reminder of a former partition in the Lower Field. Some of the landmarks had intriguing names such as Deadman's Bush, not far from the Red Conduit in the Upper Field. The Causeway upon the Hill—it developed into the Causey —was an upper road leading to Petersham, for the lower one was often impassable, especially during winter.

James I appointed Sir Thomas Gorges and his wife, Helena, Marchioness of Northampton—she was immortalised by Edmund Spenser, who dedicated the elegy *Daphnaïda* to her—as co-Keepers of the Palace and Park, and their names appear in the Court Rolls as the Lord and Lady of the Royal manor. The entries of present-ments or cases heard at the Court Baron reveal a clear picture of Richmond in early Stuart days.

The water, trickling down the Hill, flowed in open ditches or "shewers", and those who did not scour them as they ran past their dwellings, or who attempted to divert the course of the water, were fined heavily. The tenants of Pensioners' Alley were in trouble frequently, sometimes because they turned the water towards the "King's Green". This ancient lane, said to have acquired its quaint name because it was a favourite byway of Royal pensioners, lost its historical identity in 1903, when its derelict cottages were cleared and it was retitled Golden Court.

Charles I observed that rainwater from the Hill settled in front of the Palace and ordered the Commissioners of Sewers to find a remedy: they solved the problem by constructing a vault on the Green for which the tenants paid. This King transferred the Court Leet (dealing with petty crimes) from Kingston-upon-Thames to Richmond. The Richmond people begged him to release them from their subjection to that town and reminded him that Kingston "skymmeth awaie the Creame from His Majestie"—the fines. That argument won the day.

The Court Rolls prove how effectively trouble-makers were dealt with in those times: in September 1605, for example, Mary Crome was threatened with a fine of forty shillings if she did not remove from her house the Widow Lathewaight, "because the said Widow is a common scould". Nicholas Awstrell, declared to be a "Common Eave-Dropper", was fined five shillings. Sometimes arguments between tenants were so involved that they could not be settled such as, "touching the Business between Mr. Brabant and Mr. Lovell We hear nothing but words so we leave it as we find it". Strangers were unwelcome in case they became a communal burden and the Select Vestry of the Parish Church, formed in 1614, presently assisted in eliminating newcomers, for they ordered that "Mr. Thorpe, Mr. Cross and Mr. Roane should goe from house to house and take notice of all strangers", who then were removed speedily.

Repeated threats of punishments to those who washed clothes within ten feet of the Well (the Conduit) on the Backside of the Church in the Upper Common Field, proved that this was a favourite habit, hard to break. Fishing, without the general consent of the tenants, in the four local ponds was forbidden. The Town Pond occupied the site of the present Dome Buildings in the Quadrant.

Those who lived near the deserted "Fryars" were checked when they tried to encroach upon its site and fishermen were told that they must not hang up their nets or store their boats on the ancient precincts. A Treasury account of 1611 indicates that the ground of the Convent of Observant Friars was levelled, although some sections of the buildings must have been left standing. The same

8   Richmond: The Parish Church of St. Mary Magdalene

9   Petersham: The Interior of St. Peter's Church

10   The Thames at Richmond, showing the Palace (c. 1629)

From the painting by David Vinkeboons

document refers to Inigo Jones's estimate for piling, planking and bricking three aits in the Thames at Richmond. These little islands were much larger than they are today, for tidal action has worn away their soil. The tenants who inhabited them paid a low rent, but on their decease the Lord of the Royal manor claimed a young swan from their heirs.

Solomon de Caux, the French architect, worked for Henry, Prince of Wales, who maintained his own household in Richmond Palace, where he finished his education in peaceful surroundings. The Frenchman designed a picture gallery for the Prince, who is credited with founding the present Royal Collection, and he devised some ingenious waterworks for the gardens in which his young patron took great interest. Henry's ideas on horticulture were influenced, no doubt, by Sir Francis Bacon, who recently had sold his estate, Twickenham Park, where he had cultivated its grounds.

The Prince of Wales endeared himself to local farmers, for when he hunted he made his followers respect their cornfields. The King's shipwright, Phineas Pett, built him a small vessel, *The Disdain*, which, carved, painted and rigged, ensigns and pennants flying, was a charming sight as it sailed up and down the Thames. His sister, Princess Elizabeth, who became the Queen of Bohemia and the ancestress of the House of Hanover, lived at Kew and brother and sister spent happy days, hunting in the Royal Park.

The promising young Prince died tragically and swiftly at the age of eighteen: he had been warned that his fondness for swimming in the Thames at night was injurious to his health, but he had refused to abandon the practice. The new Prince of Wales, the future Charles I, in his turn, "set up housekeeping in Richmond Palace". In addition to rearing his sons in the home of his Tudor predecessors, James I used it as a breeding-ground for pheasants. Horace Busino, employed by the Venetian ambassador, thought the birds interesting when he saw them in a small orchard beneath the Palace windows. Some were pied red, others were white and "very handsome" and as they were in unroofed wooden compartments, their wings were clipped.

King James had another interest in the neighbourhood, for in 1619, he granted an annual subsidy to Sir Francis Crane, who established tapestry works on the site of the deceased Dr. Dee's laboratory in Mortlake. Fifty Flemish weavers were imported and Francis Cleyn, a native of Rostock, directed the designs. The tapestries soon became famous on the Continent and the future of the young industry seemed brilliant. But the factory was affected unfavourably by the Civil War, and never reverted to its first successful phase, closing after about eighty years' existence.

London was plague-swept almost as soon as Charles I ascended the Throne and some of the Government Departments, including the Exchequer and the Records, were evacuated to Richmond. The King and his bride, Queen Henrietta Maria, stayed at Hampton Court but they visited Richmond frequently, for the King had granted apartments in the Palace to the French ambassador, the Duc de Chevreuse. His Duchesse, a leader of fashion, gave birth to a daughter at Richmond and the King and Queen attended the child's christening. That summer the versatile young mother swam across the Thames one evening, a daring exploit that caused the local people to nickname her "The Female Leander".

When the Royal children appeared, Richmond was used as a nursery and once again the Palace was known as "The Prince's Court". In 1634, Justices of the Peace, requested to suppress some of Surrey's inns, licensed a number of taverns in the Royal manor, stating as their reason that it had become "a place of much resort and recreation for divers gentlemen and citizens". The "Red Lyon", enjoying one of its successful phases, was the centre of an unusual ceremony in 1638, when William Crowne was created Rouge Dragon, Pursuivant of Arms. The Earl Marshal closed the proceedings by pouring a bowl of wine over the new Rouge Dragon's head. In Charles I's reign, the "Castle" tavern opened in a gabled house near the Town Pond, and although it does not function in its original premises, it has known over three hundred years of local history.

2

The Prince's Court attracted elegant young men to Richmond and, the spectre of the coming Civil War as yet hidden, they dallied with pretty women on the banks of this Arcadia-on-Thames.

Indeed, "the place was so fatal for love, that never any dis-
engaged young person went thither, who returned again free".
So a law student, John Hutchinson, was warned when he told his
friends he was going to spend the summer in the house of Charles
Coleman who directed a School of Music close to Richmond
Palace. John thought it was a joke, but a few weeks later he recalled
the warning and began to think there must be some magic in the
place which enchanted men, for he had fallen deeply in love with
an unknown woman.

At the School of Music he was introduced to a young Mistress
Apsley, tabled for practice of her lute during the absence of her
mother from Richmond. Lady Apsley was paying a country visit
with her elder daughter Lucy for the purpose of arranging a marriage
for the girl.

John heard much about this elder sister as he escorted young
Mistress Apsley home: she showed him the Latin books clever
Lucy read and he was impressed by a song Lucy had composed.
He deeply regretted that he had not met this elder sister, who began
to absorb his thoughts. At last a message came to say that Lady
Apsley and her daughter were coming home and that Lucy was a
bride. When John heard the news he turned "pale as ashes", and
almost fainted. But the rumour of her marriage was false, and as
soon as she returned to Richmond he contrived to meet her. She
fulfilled his expectations and despite their friends' opposition, he
wooed her swiftly and successfully. On the day that arrangements
for their wedding were concluded, Lucy contracted smallpox, and
when she had recovered her face was so marred that people were
afraid to look at her. But John married her immediately and took
her away from the place "so fatal for love". He became the Colonel
Hutchinson who signed Charles I's death-warrant.

Two artists left impressions of Richmond in the early Stuart
period. David Vinkeboons' delightful painting (now in the Fitzwilliam Museum, Cambridge) shows an attractive vista of the
river, the grey façade of the Palace gleaming in the distance, and in
the Town (now Water) Lane, the red-tiled gables of the "Feathers"
(10). Higher up, we see the Ferry, and then the Hill, by this time fringed
with houses. The Thames is lively with pleasure craft and swans

glide near a boat. In the foreground, on the Twickenham bank, the sylvan atmosphere is emphasised by a group of cavaliers and well-attired women, who have alighted from a coach. They watch the performance of Morris dancers who have brought a hobby-horse. A dog barks as one of the dancers collects coins from the bystanders, holding out a long-handled spoon.

Wenceslaus Hollar drew the Palace from the Twickenham bank, presenting the same aspect as Wyngaerde had done eighty odd years earlier. Slight changes can be noted and in Hollar's work we see a wharf and crane, which were used to remove timber from the Royal Park. It stood at the spot where the railway bridge now spans the river, and here, at the end of the seventeenth century, Huguenot refugees established a calico printing works, one of the first of its kind to be founded in England.

Hollar made a second etching—this time he went to the Hill summit, crowned by a windmill which stood on the site of the present "Morshead" Hotel. Thomas Mercer was granted the land for this "grist mill" in April 1621, and it functioned for a century—Richmond's fields grew chiefly corn. The artist's interest, however, centred on a cavalcade of men and women who rode towards the King's New Park (now Richmond Park).

Charles I created the New Park, despite bitter opposition, the anxiety of the City of London and against the advice of his Ministers. Many houses and farms had to be demolished before the scheme could be carried through, and for these the King offered favourable payment. Most of the owners agreed to sell, but some demurred and one man refused firmly to yield his estate, but he was obliged to capitulate.

Before negotiations were concluded for these properties, the wall was begun and Edward Manning was paid the first of the many thousands of pounds that passed through his hands, to rail in coppices, cut lawns and make ponds and a river. Concessions were made to the public, rights of way were guaranteed and poor people were allowed to go into the New Park and gather firewood. Charles I hunted there for the last time in August 1647—he killed a stag and a buck and then dined with his younger children at Syon House before his gaolers escorted him back to Hampton Court.

By 1640 dark clouds had gathered on the national horizon, and the Privy Council, expressing fears concerning the safety of the Royal children at Richmond, and alarmed by the "traitorous insolence lately practised by some base people near Southwark", ordered Surrey's trained bands to guard the Palace day and night. It was an uneasy year, for the plague was rampant in the neighbour-hood and its terrors were described by Cornelius Holland, Paymaster to the Royal children, in a letter to Sir Harry Vane at Whitehall. Begging for the immediate removal of his charges to a safer place, he stated: "It hath pleased God to visit the town of Richmond with the plague in two houses near the pond at the entrance of the town, two died this forenoon full of tokens out of one house and two more out of another house this afternoon since Dr. Chambers was with the King and another child now lies sick whom we fear is infected from those other houses and indeed we suspect all this to have happened from the barber's man of the tent who died in one of these houses. . . ."

The Royal children were sent to Oatlands and the Richmond Parish Registers prove that during the late summer the plague claimed many victims.

Chapter V

CROMWELLIAN INTERLUDE

Parliamentary Surveyors and "The Account"—Sir Gregory Norton—Local Disagreements—Dr. Duppa—Henry Carter

I

IN December 1649, the Parliamentary surveyors, among whom appears the name of John Webb, signed "The Account", their valuation of the Royal manor of Richmond, owned by Charles Stuart, late King of England. A Member of Parliament, Mr. Laurence, sent to the Palace by the New Rulers to watch their interests, occupied apartments near the Gatehouse, while others, chiefly in the gallery, were used by Robert Roane, who had been appointed Underkeeper of the House by the deceased king. Roane's courage was greater than his loyalty to his late master, for finding that, "he hath carried himself fayrely to the Parliament", the surveyors commended him in the Account, adding that he had risked his life to extinguish a fire in the Wardrobe. Scorched beams, relics of this fire, were discovered during alterations to the house made this century.

The Palace had been stripped of its treasures, with the help of Clement Kynnersley, Yeoman of the Wardrobe of Beds to Charles I. Kynnersley, who had an estate in Richmond, played a curious rôle in the Civil War. He received one hundred pounds to prepare Richmond Palace for the captive king, who refused to go there. He made himself useful to the Parliamentary men in assem‐ bling the Royal *objets d'art*, and he was mentioned approvingly in the Council's Orders of the Day, for his services in "discovering the late King's goods". At the Restoration Charles II reappointed him Yeoman of the Wardrobe of Beds, possibly because he knew the whereabouts of the tapestries and pictures that the King was anxious to recover. Kynnersley died in 1662 and his grave is marked by an altar tomb outside the Parish Church.

The Parliamentary surveyors tramped over every yard of the

Palace, measuring and assessing. They admired the domestic planning, the Great Buttery, the Saucery, the Silver Scullery, all convenient to the Great Hall, where they made a note that the clock in the case with a large bell had a "fayre dial or finger". (Charles I had commissioned David Ramsay, first Master of the Clockmakers' Company, to make and install a new clock with a gilded dial at Richmond.) They observed that the Privy Lodgings had fourteen turrets which were very "perspicacious to the landscape around": they appraised the freestone, the bricks, the abundance of useful lead.

They were pleased with the furnishings in the Chapel Royal, counted the steps of the Canted Tower—this, they considered the chief "Ornament unto the whole Fabrick of Richmond Court". They roamed into the Privie Garden where the beds were arranged like a round knot divided into four quarters, bordered with box. In the centre of the knot they saw a "fayr Ewe-Tree"—this yew was alive in the nineteenth century, and was over ten feet in circumfer-ence. They took a census of the fruit-trees, mentioned a little pigeon-house in the Housekeeper's Yard and a handsome round turtle-dove cage, partly wired and partly covered with blue slate. They went beyond the two long galleries to "The Fryars", which, used as a chandler's shop, contained seven rooms. They valued the materials in the Palace and its gardens at ten thousand, seven hundred and eighty-two pounds, nineteen shillings and twopence.

They measured Richmond Green and found it contained twenty acres: today, including the Little Green, it comprises eleven and a half acres. They found it well turfed, and forty-eight of its one hundred and thirteen elm trees stood in a handsome walk on the west side. They went into the Little Park (the Royal Park by the river was known by that name to distinguish it from the New Park on the Hill, not known then as Richmond Park). Dean Colet's Lodge was in a good condition and fit for habitation, but there were no deer in the Park, and for the most part the trees were "ould Dotrells and decayed pollard good for little save the fier".

In 1650 the Palace was sold to Thomas Rookesby, William Goodwin and Adam Baynes, who disposed of it for ten thousand pounds to Sir Gregory Norton, the regicide who had signed Charles I's death-warrant and who was collecting Royal treasures.

Sir Gregory, the new Lord of the manor, soon came into conflict with the leading tenants. First he announced that he intended to build a brick wall in front of the Palace, to replace Queen Elizabeth's chequer-rail which had rotted twenty years beforehand and had never been repaired. When the matter was discussed at a Court Baron—according to traditional custom the tenants of a manor were the judges and were able to check the Lord's tyranny—it was protested that this wall would exclude them from part of the Green, hitherto opened to them. Other disadvantages from which they suffered under the new régime were mentioned. They complained that a farmer, or farmers, had straightened the usual cartway to Kew and there had been an attempt to take from them the footway to Brentford. But their greatest grievance was that the track to the Thames (now Old Palace Lane), an "antient passage", had been incorporated into the Little Park and they could not reach the wharf.

Four years later they protested again that Sir Gregory, or his agents had debarred them from this old footway to the river, but soon after this last complaint the regicide died and his widow, Dame Martha Norton became Lady of the manor. She gave the tenants a new Lord for she married Robert, Lord Gordon, Viscount Kenmure.

2

Entries in the Court Rolls during the Protectorate years indicate unusual local disagreements and resentments. Thomas Cockdell or Cogdell (the spelling varies in the records) was fined repeatedly for removing and converting to his own use the ducking-, or as it was referred to at times, the "cucking"-stool; the wooden chair fixed to the end of a long beam in which scolds, quarrelsome married couples and sometimes dishonest tradesmen, were forced to sit while they were plunged in cold water. In 1652 Cockdell was ordered to replace the ducking-stool in its customary position by the Town Pond, or pay a ten-shilling fine. He did not obey and two years later he was threatened with a fine of five, then six pounds, and finally began a series of demands from him of thirty-nine shillings each. Another ducking-stool appeared by the Town Pond, but we do not know if Cogdell gave way: his obstinacy indicates that

11 "A View of Kew", showing Kew Green and the first Kew Bridge
in the mid-eighteenth century

From a contemporary print

12 "Sir Charles Asgill's Villa with a View of the Bridge at Richmond", about 1790

From an engraving by Thomas Malton

13 The (rebuilt) Duppa Almshouses, with their mid-seventeenth-century Gateway

14 The Bentley Monument (*c.* 1666) in the Parish Church

RICHMOND

he was a man with progressive ideas, and protested against the crude method of punishment.

John Bentley was amerced for "detaining the Hommage Book" which he refused to give up, and the Homage—the tenants who formed the jury at the Court Baron—found themselves at a great disadvantage, for it contained indispensable information. This was another singular case for Bentley, a well-to-do tenant, was a Vestry-man and sometime Churchwarden. When he died in 1660 he desired to be buried in Richmond Parish Church "under my owne pewe . . ." and ordered his executor to erect a monument of alabaster and black marble that was to cost at least fifty pounds. His bust can be seen there today, his expression grim, his chin determined and his nose somewhat worn by time (14).

Other people were affected by social changes. In 1650 a Richmond schoolmaster, Robert Mossom, was sequestered and forbidden to teach because, against the new regulations, he had read the Book of Common Prayer. He was unemployed for six years and then, in despair, sent a petition to Oliver Cromwell, pointing out that he had taught diligently and had never acted against the Government, but had been deprived of earning a living to maintain his wife and six small children. His courage was rewarded, for he was given per-mission to return to his schoolmastering.

During the Protectorate years, Dr. Brian Duppa, former tutor to Charles II, lived in retirement in Richmond. He owned land by the river and his house probably occupied the site of the cinema near Water Lane. He surrendered some of his local property to his friend, Sir Justinian Isham, and the twain secretly communicated with a network of Royalists centred in Petersham. Duppa managed to evade the attention of the Government until a few months before the Restoration and then Major Audley was instructed to search his house for papers, persons and alms; to discover from him with whom he had discussed the present designs of the enemy, and to make him promise to stay in his home. He survived the dangers and became Bishop of Winchester after the Restoration.

The old people in Richmond used to relate a tradition they had heard from their forbears. Noticing that he was followed by soldiers, Duppa rushed into a cottage and begged the housewife to hide him. She made him get into a bed and cover himself with clothes, contriving to get rid of the men when they knocked at the door, on the pretext that she had a sick daughter. The grateful prelate vowed he would repay her kindness.

And he did so, as a group of splendid almshouses for old women in the Vineyard prove, for he bequeathed the money for their foundation. Originally they were situated on the Hill on the site of the present Downe Terrace, but they were re-erected in the nineteenth century(13). The massive central archway, supported by Baroque stone columns, which divides the building, and the stone dressing were removed from the first almshouse with the stone gateway. The words *Deo et Carolo, Votiva Tabula* appear in the pediment over the gate with the gilt inscription: I will pay the vows which I made to God in my trouble.

Three of the Duppa Almshouses were shattered by a bomb in 1940, but they have been restored and the inmates enjoy improved accommodation. On the other side of the road we see the Michel Almshouses, founded by Humphrey Michel of Richmond Green, in 1695, and increased by his nephew John in the next century. They, too, have been rebuilt but they are grouped round a charming old-world garden and the scrolled plaque over the inscription tablet in the centre block is a picturesque reminder of bygone centuries.

In 1651, William Leaver was fined for driving his cart, laden with stones, from the Great House—as the Palace was described at the time—across the Green. He was prosecuted because his cart-wheels cut ruts in the turf, but the case is a pointer that materials were being removed at that date from the precincts. The Vestry accounts for the same year show that Leaver was paid, among other items, one pound, nine shillings, for conveying "nine load of gravel and stones to Brewers Layne and Church Layne".

But it was the surveyor, Henry Carter, who gave Henry VII's Palace its death blow, for according to evidence given by Elizabeth Smollett soon after the Restoration, he was "the first puller down of the King's House". When the return of the exiled Stuarts was in sight, the destruction occurred in a wholesale fashion for Carter sold one thousand pounds' worth of materials from the building to raise troops to fight the Royalists.

Carter had made the most of his opportunities for self-advancement during the Protectorate years. He built himself a house on the site of the tennis court near the long gallery. He was a nuisance to the tenants: he attempted to alter "an Antient Footway (Friars Lane) leading from the Thames thro' part of the Fryars which hath layn open Time out of Mind between the Court wall and the Widow Lovell's house to Richmond Green". He destroyed a brick arch connected with the water system so that the water flowing from the Hill to the Friars, was diverted from its usual course, and caused discomfort to bypassers. He left Richmond shortly before the Restoration, and that same year a loyal Royal servant asked to be allowed to live rent free in the house he had vacated. But the surveyor had feathered his nest by buying Charles I's treasures, and later notified the new Government that he had these in his possession. They included a naked Venus, one foot tall, for which he had paid Inigo Jones's pupil, John Webb, twenty pounds. He suggested to the authorities that as he, Carter, was a poor man, the vendors of the articles he had acquired should be ordered to return him the money he had paid for them and he would keep them safe until they were collected.

Chapter VI

AFTER THE RESTORATION

I

THE second period of Richmond's subject ownership was over, but the reports that Charles II received from the Surveyor-General on the state of his boyhood's home were unfavourable. Twenty-seven householders occupied the Royal ten acres —some lived in the decaying ruins or had restored falling outhouses. Even the ground of the Chapel Royal was being used. Some of these undesired tenants like the widow Joane West, who had expended five hundred pounds in repairing the former flesh and pastry larders which comprised her dwelling, petitioned the King to allow them to remain, and Crown leases on the site date from this period.

It is believed that when the Lady of the manor, Charles I's widow, Queen Henrietta Maria, returned to the derelict Palace she occupied the sections of the building we see today. She wandered sadly through the few surviving rooms, but the place depressed her and she departed for ever, leasing the Royal manor to Edward Villiers.

He was related to the King's favourite, Lady Castlemaine who, at times, found Richmond a convenient place for a quick retreat. On July 16th, 1662, the diarist Samuel Pepys wrote: "This day I was told that my Lady Castlemaine, being quite fallen out with her husband, did yesterday go away from him, with all her plate, jewels and other best things; and is gone to Richmond to a brother of her's; which, I am apt to think, was a design to get out of town, that the King might come at her the better." We can imagine Pepys's smiles as on July 22nd, 1663, he entered: "In discourse of the ladies at Court, Captain Ferrers tells me that my Lady Castlemaine is now as great as ever she was; and that her going away was only a fit of

15   Sudbrook Lodge, Ham Common

16   Montrose House, Petersham: Built about 1670 and added to
in the eighteenth century

17 The "Chinese Chippen-
dale" Overmantel in the
Drawing-room

18 The Staircase, showing Plaster
Decoration on Wall

19 The Entrance Hall, Panelled in Scotch Fir

RUTLAND LODGE, PETERSHAM

20 The Queen's Bedchamber, believed to have been used by Catherine of Braganza

21 The Great Staircase, 1638

22 The North Door, a Reproduction
of the Original

HAM HOUSE

24   Petersham House, built about 1670 and added to in
the eighteenth century

23   Rutland Lodge, built about 1666 and enlarged in 1720

AT PETERSHAM

her own upon some slighting words of the King, so that she called for her coach at a quarter of an hour's warning, and went to Rich-mond; and the King the next morning, under pretence of going a-hunting, went to see her and make friends, and never was a-hunting at all."

According to a local tradition, the other Royal favourite, Nell Gwynn, lived in Sudbrook Lodge, the square house with the steep, hipped, tiled roof that stands on the edge of Ham Common (15). Many of the leading houses in Petersham originated in the late Stuart period, although in the next century, they were extended, storeys added, and they were given Georgian characteristics. We associate them with Restoration times, but their internal features evolved gradually at a later age.

This was the case with Petersham House on the main road to Kingston, its entrance door distinguished by a Regency circular domed portico upheld by Ionic columns (24). It was built about 1670 for Colonel Thomas Panton, Keeper of the New Park, and in those days it had a sloping roof with dormers. Its interior is characterised by immense paintings executed by Laguerre, who also adorned the neighbouring Whitton House for Kneller. He decor-ated the hall, the hall ceiling and a landing of Petersham House with classical figures, and great gods and buxom goddesses are outlined in a background that has become misty and blue with time. A lower stair soffit is treated charmingly with cherubs which hold a diadem of stars over mythological lovers.

Some of the rooms in this handsome house have Adam mantel-pieces and two are executed in white marble and blue john, the latter reminiscent of an uncut amethyst. The mantelpiece at one end of the long music-room is finished with a centre plaque, sculptured with the figures of St. Cecilia and her attendants, their instruments and music reproduced in intricate detail. The music-room leads to a small boudoir and here the mantelpiece is represen-tative of the work of Flaxman and Wedgwood. The motif of the Virtuous Woman is attractively illustrated in the blue oval cameos.

During the mid-eighteenth century, the Rutland family lived in Petersham House and from that time the adjoining mansion has been known as Rutland Lodge (23). It dates, however, from about

1666 when it was built by Sir William Bolton, a Lord Mayor of London. It was owned a few years later by a famous lawyer, Sir John Darnall, whose monogram is encircled in the wrought-iron gate. He died in 1735 and alterations were made to the house about 1720, when a wing was added and a storey was placed above the rich cornice. A bell dated 1668 was removed from the roof when it was reconstructed: a copper-lined boiler in the cellar, placed near an old cider-press, shows original brickwork, and the cornbin in the disused stables is panelled.

The entrance hall is panelled in Scotch fir, and the heavy markings indicate that the trees were grown in a cold climate. The hall now comprises the original dining-room, and the ceiling is divided by an arch with carved spandrels, flanked on either side by fluted pilasters. The bracket-ends of the stairs are carved, the soffits moulded. The first-floor walls and the ceiling above are plastered delicately with festoons and medallions, enclosing classical heads. The egg and tongue moulding which borders the wall decoration is repeated on the door panels. The central feature of the drawing-room is the Chinese Chippendale carving over the chimney-breast, its scrolls enclosing a bird.

Rutland Lodge expresses the Age of Elegance, the mark of careful, detailed craftsmanship which touched Petersham in the early eighteenth century. This reappears in the house across the road, Montrose House (16), called after the Duchess who occupied it. It was built by Darnall's father-in-law, Sir Thomas Jenner, who was another notable lawyer, but it has been altered and extended. In the days when these houses appeared, Lady Darnall could see plainly what was happening in her parents' home, for no busy main road with its stream of traffic divided them. Travellers to Kingston turned before they came to the "Plough", now the "Dysart Arms", and the green track which ran from Richmond Hill ended by the present "Fox and Duck". Here stood the stocks and the pound, and just past Montrose House was the village maypole, ordered to be removed in 1716, because it was rotten and dangerous to pedestrians. Modern Petersham is characterised by narrow lanes which were formed when the owners of the great houses built high brick walls round their grounds.

Petersham was invaded by craftsmen in the late Stuart period, for in addition to all this building in the village, the Duke and Duchess of Lauderdale enlarged and redecorated Ham House. Today this is one of Surrey's show-places, for the late Sir Lyonel Tollemache presented it to the National Trust in 1948; the Government bought its contents and the Victoria and Albert Museum arranged it to emphasise the Carolean note.

Ham House (20-22, 25), an H-shaped mansion, built in 1610 for Sir Thomas Vavasour, was acquired in the sixteen-thirties by William Murray, former whipping-boy and Groom of the Bedchamber to Charles I. The King granted him the manors of Petersham and Ham and invested him with an earldom and as his father had been rector of Dysart, Fifeshire, he took the title of Dysart. The first earl had no sons and his daughter, Elizabeth, who became Countess of Dysart in her own right, inherited Ham House. Her first husband was Sir Lionel Tollemache of Helmingham Hall, Suffolk, the founder of the family who lived at Ham House for nearly three hundred years. Elizabeth Tollemache, who was on most friendly terms with Oliver Cromwell, fell in love with the Duke of Lauderdale. Sir Lionel and Lauderdale's wife both died conveniently, and the widow and widower were married in Petersham Church in 1672.

As we pass through the main door of Ham House, we step into Vavasour's Great Hall, the floor checked in black and white marble. In the next century the centre of the hall ceiling was removed and its sides formed the floor of the Round Gallery, a picture gallery. This is reached by the Great Staircase installed by William Murray, in which the balustrade is composed of pierced panels, carved with trophies of arms, the newels shaped like baskets of fruit. Originally the panels were picked out with gold, but later generations had the staircase coated heavily with brown paint.

Two significant portraits stand out among the canvases in the Round Gallery. One, painted by Sir Peter Lely (who lived at Kew) depicts Elizabeth Tollemache as a radiant young woman. There is nothing here to indicate the character Bishop Burnet gave her in his *History of my own Time*: "nor was there anything she stuck at to compass her end, for she was violent in everything—a violent friend, and a much more violent enemy". Lely's portrait of the young Elizabeth shows a woman of great beauty, her eyes intelligent, her expression mild, her golden hair touching her white neck, the bodice of her shimmering blue satin finished with tiny pearly buttons.

At the end of the Round Gallery there is another portrait, labelled "Both Ye Graces in one Picture". This, painted shortly before Lely's death, portrays the Lauderdales, a middle-aged couple, sitting on a carved garden bench, similar to the one now placed near the front entrance. The Duke looks arrogant, contemptuous, self-satisfied: the Duchess, her features coarsened, her faded hair carelessly dressed, has a cynical, amused expression as if she had found life a grand joke.

The ambitious pair enlarged Ham House by extending it and enclosing the space between the wings on the south side. This gave them a series of additional, but in some cases extremely small apartments, which despite their size, were embellished with studied elaboration. Money poured from the Lauderdale coffers into the hands of foreign artists and craftsmen. Two of the ceilings were decorated by Verrio—the alcove in the Duchess's bedroom is a charming example of his art in miniature form. Some ceilings were plastered with laurel wreath ovals, the spandrels intricately treated; laurels appear in gilded cornices and are entwined with the ducal coronet in parquet floors.

Artists were commissioned to paint pictures especially to fit spaces above doorcases, of which seascapes by van de Velde the Younger are notable examples. The wall hangings were sumptuous and those of brown and gilt leather we see in the Marble Dining-Room, have been there since the Lauderdales' day. An ebony table, Elizabeth Dysart's monogram visible in its silver mounts, the legs modelled as caryatides, is placed in the tiny Miniature Room, which leads to the Long Gallery that formed part of the original house.

Persian carpets, lacquer pieces, Mortlake tapestries poured into the Lauderdales' home in an incessant shower: the last prodigal gesture was the introduction of silver chimney furniture—chased tongs, shovels, brushes, bellows and pans. These still gleam in white

25   Ham House, built originally in 1610

26   Petersham: The Cole Monument (*c.* 1624) in St. Peter's Church

fireplaces, harmonious among the rippling colour fantasies, the brocade and velvet upholstery. Much of the furniture seen at Ham House today was mentioned in an inventory made in 1679, although metal threads are tarnished, vivid tones slightly subdued. Since this inventory was taken, two "sleeping-chayres", carved, gilded, and with rachets for adjusting the backs, have stood in the same position in the Queen's Closet. This tiny apartment, leading from the Queen's Bedchamber—probably it was occupied at some time by Catherine of Braganza—is the most elaborately decorated in the house. Ganymede and the Eagle look down from a painted oval in the ceiling: fireplace surround and window-sill are finished with scagliola inlaid with colours, believed to be the earliest example of this composition in England.

Nothing was forgotten: the Lauderdales were out to impress their associates and they had their reward when John Evelyn recorded in his diary that their home was "like a great Prince's". The grounds he admired with their fountains, statues and orangeries, may have lost some of their ornaments, but on a summer's day they remain a place of enchantment, "at the banks of the sweetest river in the world".

Doubtless the Duchess, who died in 1698, could have answered a baffling question—was Charles I's soldier nephew, Prince Rupert of Bavaria, married to Lady Francis Bard? And did this marriage take place in Petersham Church, or in Ham House chapel? Prince Rupert was presumed to have died a bachelor, but his attachment to Lady Frances, by whom he had a son, was well known. A document, dated 1664, signed by Henry Bignell, Minister, has come to light in modern times, certifying that he married this couple at Petersham, Surrey. There was a Minister of that name in the village in 1658 and in 1666, but this evidence cannot be corroborated by the Parish Registers, because pages are missing for the period indicated. They appear, indeed, to have been cut deliberately and the subject remains one of history's fascinating mysteries.

John Evelyn, who admired Ham House and its grounds, was often in the neighbourhood, for this connoisseur of gardens was interested in the horticultural experiments conducted by Sir Henry, later Lord Capel of Kew. In his opinion Capel produced the finest fruits in England and he was much impressed by the way in which he was "contriving very high palisadoes of reeds to shade his oranges during the summer and painting those reeds in oil". He thought his orangery and myrtetum most beautiful and well kept—Capel paid five pounds each for his white striped hollies and gave forty pounds for two lentisks.

The diarist had other friends in the district—one was Charles II's Cofferer, Mr., later Lord Brouncker, who had leased the "Abbey of Sheen, formerly a Monastery of Carthusians, there yet remaining one of their solitary cells with a cross". Sir William Temple, who had married Dorothy Osborne after his long courtship, also lived in the hamlet of West Sheen, and found gardening a fascinating hobby: Evelyn noted how exquisitely his wall-fruit trees were nailed and trained. There was a pretty little girl in Temple's household— Hester Johnson, born in Richmond in 1681, the daughter of a woman employed by Sir William's sister, Lady Gifford. She was given her first lessons by Temple's secretary, Jonathan Swift, and his attachment to the girl whom he immortalised in his *Journal to Stella*, dated from those days.

Evelyn recommended his friend John Aubrey, compiler of the *Natural History and Antiquities of the County of Surrey*, to visit Richmond and its neighbourhood. Aubrey went to Petersham which he described as "formerly a priviledg'd Place, as is plain from Records in the Tower of London, so that none could be arrested here, or one arrested at any other Place could not be brought through this Place, but through long and scandalous Neglect this valuable Privilege is lost". He explored St. Peter's, the Parish Church and found it was "but very small". Despite alterations in subsequent centuries, St. Peter's has remained diminutive. Tucked away down a lane, set among river meadows, its red bricks and little tower have an old-world air, as if the churchwarden who spent five pounds in arranging mourning in the church when Queen Anne died, had only just submitted his account to the Vestry.

A Saxon church stood there first, and that was replaced by a Norman one—there is Norman stone-work in the chancel wall and a blocked-up lancet window. The interior has retained its high box-pews and it has a neat gallery(9). Its walls are studded with tablets which recall the days when Petersham was regarded as the most aristocratic village in the kingdom. The Cole monument is set in the north wall of the chancel (26). George Cole, who died in 1624, and was Recorder in the Augmentation Office of the Middle Temple, owned the Elizabethan manor-house, the first Petersham Lodge, which stood in the present Petersham Park. The effigy of the lawyer in his long black gown, a cap on his head, a parchment in his hand, is placed above that of his wife whose neck is encircled by an enormous ruff. They lie in an arched recess guarded by black Corinthian columns and at the base is the tiny effigy of George Cole junior, who died at the age of four a few days before the decease of his illustrious grandfather.

Aubrey went on to Richmond and gazed gloomily at the ruined Palace. "But Henry VII built Richmond a splendid and magnifi-cent House, which was after the most exquisite Way of Architec-ture", he wrote, "as Henry VII's Chapel at Westminster: 'twas Pity it was spoil'd in Times of Usurpation, it is since a little repair'd." He criticised the Duppa Almshouses somewhat spitefully. "But he hath paid his Vows but poorly. Here are 10 Poor Widows who are allow'd 5 Groats a Week a piece and Twenty Shillings to buy Coals and a Gown once in two years. The Minister and Church-Wardens are Overseers of it. But because they are Alms-Women they are not to have any Benefit from the Parish and so they live in a starving condition."

Had Aubrey written about contemporary aspects, doubtless he would have observed that the Green was cheerful with "crickett-players", and that Charles II had given the tenants a bowling-green which extended from what is now the Little Green to the Old Vicarage. The tenants built a brick wall round it and William Drew, who was responsible for its turf, rented it for a small annual sum which was devoted to the poor in the parish. (It is believed that he was empowered to charge players a small fee.) The Drew family held it until 1733, and in the following year Queen Caroline converted it into a flower-garden, agreeing at the same time to pay ten guineas a year as compensation. In 1765, George III enclosed the former bowling-green as part of Richmond Gardens, continuing his grandmother's annual payments. This money was paid until

1844 by the Office of Woods and Forests and then, in lieu of rent, a sum was invested in Government Stock. It now yields eight pounds, ten shillings a year and is devoted to improvements in local public recreation grounds, notably the Grove Road Park.

Before the seventeenth century closed, the Richmond Wells opened in the waste land between the Hill and the Petersham Road. The spring which supplied the medicinal waters of the Wells was referred to by Benjamin Allen, author of *Natural History of the Chalybeate Waters of England* (1699): in his opinion, "this water purgeth well but I think scarce so much as Epsom or Acton but more smoothly". Assembly Rooms soon appeared in the Wells grounds, and varied amusements were provided for those who came to drink the curative waters. At their inception the novel concerts and the dances held there were extremely fashionable and tickets were sold at London's leading coffee-houses.

Visitors who came to Richmond to drink the water were supplied with asses' milk by John Scott, who owned two hundred asses and rented them to those who wished to keep them in their homes. His imposing business card was engraved with the Royal Arms and announced his establishment as "King William's Royal Ass-House a little above ye ferry on Richmond Hill."

3

As the seventeenth century ended large areas of waste land were given to those who wished to develop them. The growth of population at this period was rapid, and was emphasised by necessary continual enlargements made in the Church of St. Mary Magdalene. Alterations, indeed, were effected in the Parish Church repeatedly during subsequent centuries and today only a fine Tudor arch remains of the original interior; the body of the church, standing against a square tower of flint and stone, preserves an historical rather than an architectural interest (8). There is a fine carved oak doorhead in the Richmond Public Library: it was placed in the Parish Church in the late Stuart period and remained there until it was removed during mid-nineteenth-century reconstruction. Four of the ring of eight bells date from the Restoration years. Three were made by James Bartlet who corrected some fault in No. 4 bell because it bears the inscription:

> Lambert made me weake not fit to ring
> But Bartlet amongst the rest hath made me sing.

An entry in the Parish Registers in Charles II's reign recorded the burial of the Royalist soldier, Colonel Henry Washington. His cousin John had emigrated to the American colonies and became the ancestor of George Washington, the first President of the United States.

In 1684 the Duke of York's family had a pew in the Parish Church, for the future James II, whose daughters, Mary and Anne were educated in the Old Palace, had become the Lord of the Royal manor, and he resided there frequently.

One summer's day in 1688, the last Royal procession that Henry VII's Archway saw, arrived at the Old Palace as a cavalcade of State coaches, escorted by horse guards came to a standstill. James II had sent his ailing heir, the delicate James Francis Edward, Prince of Wales, to his country home, hoping that the Thames Valley air would restore his health. But his hopes were in vain, the child grew weaker for he was being reared on a fantastic diet. His life seemed to be flickering out until at last the desperate King agreed to a suggestion that natural methods of feeding should be tried. (James disliked wet nursing and was convinced that it had caused the deaths of other children he had lost in their infancy.)

The neighbourhood was searched and a tilemaker's wife, who lived close to the Old Palace, was selected as the suitable candidate for the post of foster-mother. She was taken so hurriedly from her cottage that she wore only a cloth petticoat, a waistcoat, old shoes and no stockings. That night she nursed her Royal charge and from that hour he recovered, to live out his long life in exile in France.

A few days later the splendid cavalcade moved to Windsor, and this time the Richmond tilemaker's wife sat in one of the coaches. She was clean and smart in her new clothes and she had been given between two and three hundred guineas, which she said she did not know how to spend.

83

Shortly before his abdication, James II commissioned Sir Christopher Wren to restore the Old Palace. This was revealed in May 1714, when John Evans, applying for the appointment of Royal bricklayer, and angered by Wren's refusal to recommend him, submitted a long petition to the Lord High Treasurer. In this document he stated he believed Wren had forgotten that in the summer before King James went away, His Majesty ordered his Palace at Richmond to be repaired and beautified. One, Drew, who was employed on it, being incapable of performing the work, Sir Christopher had employed him (Evans) till His Majesty's departure out of England when he was dismissed without receiving the least satisfaction for the same. Evans added that he was sued afterwards, not only for the materials used by his own men, but by the bricklayers concerned before him, and he had paid for the same rather than suffer the extremity of the law.

What were Wren's plans for the restoration of the Old Palace? If the monarchy had not swerved that year, would we have seen a small edition of Hampton Court on the Royal ten acres at Richmond? There are no answers to the questions.

Chapter VII

EARLY EIGHTEENTH-CENTURY DEVELOPMENT

Charity School—Its Patrons and their Homes—William Hickey—
"Prospect Of Richmond"—The Wells and the Playhouse—The
Tilemakers—The "Star and Garter"—Queen Caroline and Richmond
Gardens—Frederick, Prince of Wales—James Thomson—Sudbrook
Park—Vancouver—Richmond Park—First Kew Bridge—Sir William
Chambers—Royal Observatory

I

IN 1713 a Charity School was opened at the corner of Brewers
Lane and Great Street. The first schoolmaster was the Minister,
the Rev. Nicholas Brady (who collaborated with Nahum Tate
in a metrical version of the Psalms) and the scholars wore metal
badges inscribed with their numbers, the date the school was
founded and the word "Richmond": their seats were made from
pews removed for that purpose from the Parish Church.

This school was maintained by annual subscriptions and the list
of benefactors was headed by Queen Anne, although she did not
live in the Royal manor. Then came the names of the Duke and
Duchess of Ormonde.

The Duke of Ormonde rebuilt Dean Colet's Lodge—it stood
close to the present Kew Observatory in the Old Deer Park—in a
simple, dignified style as a rectangular, three-storied brick house.
He was in Ireland during the reconstruction, but Lord Ranelagh,
Paymaster of the Forces, referred to its progress in his correspondence
with the Duke in such passages as: "The *sachée* windows are all
bespoke and the bricks for the arches are rubbing. There is not a
Swedish marble in all London and that is the reason why your hall
is liked to be paved with other stone."

The Duke, as leader of the English Jacobites, was impeached in
1715, his estates forfeited, and he escaped to France. A number of
Richmond residents were suspected of loyalty to the exiled House of

Stuart and the Duke of Argyll ordered Major Boyd, Muster Master of the County of Surrey, to search their homes. The Duke of Ormonde's followers have always been associated with Ormond Road (formerly Row), a terrace of early eighteenth-century houses, stamped with the atmosphere of their period. The gabled house, the Rosary, has unusual door-panels on its chimney-breasts which open and reveal intriguing flights of wooden steps. In those days this house and its semi-detached neighbour, the Hollies, may have formed one dwelling, for the words "Ormond Place" are inscribed on a stone tablet inset in the bricks. The medieval arches in the Rosary cellars indicate that an earlier building occupied the site, and it has one of the mysterious underground blocked-up passages, of which there are traces in many Richmond homes.

Lady Vanderput was a prime mover in founding the Charity School. She and her husband, Sir Peter, lived at Carrington Lodge in the Marsh Gate (now the Sheen) Road, where commodious, red brick, well-appointed dwellings began to appear.

The most distinctive survivor of these is Marshgate House, built in 1699 by John Knapp, City of London haberdasher. It lies well back from the road, square and tiered with symmetrical sash windows, its steep-pitched roof interspersed with dormers, and rising above a wooden cornice. The glory of Marshgate House is its exquisitely wrought-iron gate, suggestive of Jean Tijou's work. Its centre panel shows the lyre design, and above, in the overthrow, the monogram "K" is supported by dolphin scrolls and water-leaves. At the end of the eighteenth century the house was occupied by Dr. John Moore, author of *Zeluco*, who was visited by his famous soldier son, known later as Sir John Moore of Corunna.

Lady Dorothy Capel, widow of Lord Capel of Kew, gave generously to the school and provided for it in her will with other parish schools. She died in 1721 and her monument—a pedimented stone upheld by Corinthian columns, enclosing a tent above a flaming urn—was one of the first to be placed in St. Anne's, Kew Parish Church (37). At that time the church was only a tiny chapel, opened in 1714, on the site of a disused gravel-pit on Kew Green. Queen Anne gave the land and one hundred pounds towards its erection—her Royal Arms in the gallery still recall these gifts. But the parishioners' request for timber from Richmond Park for the building was refused.

Sir Charles Hedges, Secretary of State, also subscribed to the Charity School. His house on the west side of Richmond Green became famous at the end of the eighteenth century as the home of the Fitzwilliam treasures that passed to the University of Cambridge. Hedges planted many hedges in his grounds, and a few years later John Macky, author-traveller, saw there the longest, largest and highest hedge of holly in England.

The name of Richard Hill of Hawkestone, Shropshire, appears among the Charity School's benefactors. This successful diplomat spent his last years at Richmond where he died in 1727. A plan of the Old Palace dated 1700 proves he was in possession of a site by the former Middle Court, and a bill, dated 1699 for glazing, suggests that he was building the Garden Gate House at the period. This house, its tall, centre block flanked by two low wings, appears in an engraving illustrating Grove's *Life and Times of Cardinal Wolsey* (1742).

In the mid-eighteenth century the house, owned by Mr. Lewis Way, was rebuilt and extended. An imposing pediment, supported by Portland stone columns, was added at the rear, giving the reconstructed building, as seen from the Thames, a Colonial aspect(28). Two quaint figures guarded its front entrance—little stone Tudor trumpeters—and from these the name Trumpeter's House was derived, although at times it has been called the Old Palace.

This house has been converted recently into a set of beautifully finished modern homes. Its exterior, with its long grey-green slated roof, has been carefully preserved. A new side entrance door is distinguished by masterly modern carving, hood and brackets, executed by an old Twickenham craftsman.

During the conversion a reminder that a Royal palace once stood on the site thrust itself suddenly into the daylight. First, workmen uncovered a perpendicular stone arch facing Henry VII's Archway —the original entrance to the Middle Court. This was broken into fragments and taken away. Then three smaller arches and a stone wall came to light. Probably the eighteenth-century builders found them difficult to remove so they walled them up with bricks. When I saw them during the recent alterations, these graceful arches were visible to the caps, and as the rubble was brushed off, carved foliage appeared in the spandrels. Revealed for the first time for centuries, they evoked a vision of the palace of long ago, of the cavalcade of kings and statesmen who had known them.... It was a brief impression, for once again they are hidden behind pine-panelled hall walls.

In Queen Anne's reign, Mr. Powell built a line of sedate houses (now Old Palace Terrace) at a corner of the Green, parallel with the ancient alley, Paved Court. On the site of the former Convent of Observant Friars, divided by the verge from Powell's Row, stately dwellings had appeared in the late seventeenth century. One of these, Old Friars, its bricks mellowed into a deep wall-flower red, is approached by a small sunken garden; its square entrance hall and staircase are light with striped pine and cream painted panelling. The date 1687, embossed on a lead rainwater head indicates its origin, but the year 1775 plastered on to a stair soffit commemorates major alterations. The house is built over rambling cellars, comprising a series of small cells, their doors opening into a long cloister. Doubtless they are a relic of the former Convent, for the ground has risen a few feet.

The main block of Old Friars is joined to an annexe, a long low building, where double Venetian windows overlook the Green. When we examine the walls of this wing from the back garden, we see the words "Concert Hall", painted in faint black letters. I find an explanation of this in a newspaper advertisement of 1722. E. Marriott, former proprietor of the Richmond Wells, announced that he had moved to the "Great Room on the Green", which he intended to open for the reception of "Gentlemen and Ladies". He promised concerts of "Extraordinary musick by the Masters from the Opera", and a performance on the little flute by John Baston.

Old Friars' neighbour, Old Palace Place, has a wealth of rich oak panelling. During the First World War the two houses were adapted as a Red Cross Hospital, and the workmen who cut a connecting passage, discovered that, above the ground floor, their walls were twelve inches apart. Inside Old Palace Place, they uncovered oak timber and plaster work, which can still be seen. Then, on its exterior wall, they came across strips of a sixteenth-century floral fresco. A section of this is preserved in the Richmond Public Library: the colourings have faded, but white lilies, blue convolvuluses and reseda green leaves form a bouquet on a faint pink ground. It is believed that this mural decoration adorned the inner wall of an earlier building on the Old Friars site, probably the handsome room, used as a chandler's shop, noted in 1649 by the Parliamentary surveyors.

Like the keystone over the door of Old Palace Place, a number of doorhoods in Richmond are adorned with cherub heads. The first house in Ormond Road, its door turned towards Hill Rise, owns two cherubs in a heart-shaped keystone, and others appear along the terrace. Sometimes the cherubs gaze into each other's eyes, as they are seen on three fine old doorhoods in the Kew Foot Road. Queen Anne House, No. 11, the Green, possesses twin cherubs which peer down at the carved acanthus leaves of the architrave. They have a fine setting, for this house is a recognised good example of the local architecture of the period, its steep, hipped, tiled roof rising above a richly carved oak cornice.

We like to think of the interesting people who admired the Richmond cherubs when they were new. Were they observed, for example, by Mrs. Frances Purcell, the widow of the composer, who acquired a house in the Royal manor after her husband's death? She brought the deceased Henry's music manuscripts with her and made her will in the parlour of her last home. Nicholas Sprimont, proprietor of the Chelsea Porcelain Manufactory, is another celebrity who spent his final years at Richmond. He lived on the Hill, but we have yet to discover if he adorned the house, to which he came after his retirement, with some of his best Chelsea Toys and his finest claret and turquoise porcelain. He died in 1771 and was buried in Petersham churchyard.

And then there is that mysterious man, William Hickey, who rests in his altar tomb outside the Richmond Parish Church. Was he the kind of person who saw beauty in carved cherubs over door-ways? We do not know—his personality remains evasive. Yet he was one of the town's great benefactors, and the old men and women who live in the Hickey Almshouses in the Sheen Road owe their homes to him. These imposing grey stone buildings, grouped round a green quadrangle and reminiscent of an Oxford college, were designed by Vulliamy in 1825, nearly a century after their founder's death.

Hickey was a man of property: he was a tenant of the Royal manor in 1699 and owned some of the choicest plots on Richmond Hill, but it is unknown how he acquired his land, or what was his calling. Sometimes he is confused erroneously with the gay man-about-town who wrote brilliant memoirs, but our Hickey was dead before the other was born. If they were related, and author Hickey was associated with Twickenham, he did not mention this charitable connection.

When our Hickey died in 1728, he left his estate, worth at that time about one hundred pounds a year, to be administered by four trustees. His daughter Catherine and her husband, John Stanton, were to enjoy the income during their lives, and then the money was to provide pensions for poor old men and women in the parish. He bequeathed money to the Charity School, on condition that a place could be found there to accommodate an iron chest, containing his "Writings and other things", to be accessible to his trustees. He stipulated that these guardians of his fortune were to enjoy a dinner on every anniversary of his death and the meal, to cost three pounds, was to be paid for from his estate. The rent collector—originally the Charity School master—was to receive sixpence in the pound for his work. By the early nineteenth century, the property yielded the handsome income of over five hundred pounds a year, and then it was decided to utilise it for almshouses.

There is one clue to the unknown story of this interesting man—the name "William Hickey of Richmond" appeared in a list of "decided Jacobites", collected in 1715, and published in 1745. As a non-juror, who had refused to take an oath of allegiance to George I, his property was liable to be forfeited. Somehow he managed to retain it and he made his will on July 1st, 1727, the summer George II ascended the Throne.

The Prince of Wales (the future George II) bought Ormonde

Lodge, known thereafter as Richmond Lodge, and as its accommodation was limited, in 1724 he ordered four houses to be built
by the Archway overlooking the Green, for the Princess's Maids
of Honour(27).

Finished at either end with quoins, in essentials the exteriors of the
Maids of Honour Row houses are identical. Every top storey has
recessed red panels: the storeys are divided by white string courses
and five tall sash windows on each first floor are surmounted by
ornamental keystones. Each forecourt is enclosed by wrought-iron
railings with an ornamental gate and stone balls cap the dividing
piers. Their Georgian atmosphere is dominant and is best described
in the words of Charles Dickens, who, surely, thought of one of
these houses when Pip of *Great Expectations* took Estella to Richmond,
for this is what he wrote:

"We came to Richmond all too soon, and our destination there,
was a house by the Green: a staid old house, where hoops and
powder and patches, embroidered coats, rolled stockings, ruffles,
and swords, had had their court days many a time. . . .

"A bell with an old voice—which I dare say in its time had often
said to the house, Here is the green farthingale, Here is the diamond-
hilted sword, Here are the shoes with red heels and the blue
solitaire,—sounded gravely in the moonlight, and two cherry-
coloured maids came fluttering out to receive Estella."

Local Rates Books show that the Maids inhabited their new
homes in 1728, but they do not appear to have occupied them for
many years. Presently No. 4 was tenanted by Heidegger, Manager
of the King's Theatre, the Haymarket, London, who was nicknamed "The Swiss Count". Heidegger, described as the "ugliest
man in the world", gave beauty to the house, for he commissioned
his scene-painter, Antonio Jolli, to decorate the entrance hall.

The artist painted in oil-colours on the large sunken pine panels,
on oblong panels beneath the chair rail, on the shutters, over doorcases and across the chimney-piece. In recent years heavy coats of
varnish which concealed the fine details, have been removed and the
decorations, in their Baroque frames, have recovered their pristine
charm, their pellucid greens and blues reflecting the tints of con-
trasting aquamarines.

The small panels Jolli covered with emblems of the arts and seasons: the larger ones he decorated with landscapes. Scenes that the Swiss Heidegger probably knew in his youth—the Rhine with Basle, St. Peter's Platz, Basle, and the Falls of Schaffhausen are partnered by Mediterranean views—the seaport of Naples, Vesuvius, its crater wreathed in smoke, the Tivoli and the Temple of the Sibyl, enriched by the powerful atmosphere of warm sunshine. He devoted a third series to Chinese topography—that little-known land in the Far East fascinated eighteenth-century people, who must have been intrigued by the ornamental pagoda they saw in the hall of this placid house by Richmond Green.

The paintings became well known, but the sources of their inspiration were identified only in recent years by Mr. Edward Croft Murray, the owner of No. 4. He traced their origin to Martin Zeiler's *Topographia Heluetiae* (1642), with plates by Matthias Merian, *Topographia Italiae* (1688), and to Fischer von Erlach's *Entwurff Einer Historischen Architectur.*

The engraving entitled "The Prospect of Richmond in Surrey", published by Henry Overton and J. Hook towards the end of the eigh-teen-twenties (6), shows that the two houses on the right of the Old Palace Archway—Old Court House and Wentworth House—originally closely resembled Maids of Honour Row. Old Court House has acquired a Georgian bow window and a flight of stone steps, and Wentworth House, redesigned by Laxton in the mid-nineteenth century, has lost its early characteristics. A turreted section of the Old Palace beyond these houses is conspicuous in the engrav-ing. Lady Winchelsea occupied it at the period, but some years later it was reported that part had fallen down and the site was cleared.

In the background of "The Prospect" we see the worples dividing the cornfields on the Hill: Great Street is lined with houses and gardens and at one end the "Red Lion" is distinct. The Jacobean mansion near Duke's Lane (now Duke Street and named after a William Duke) was occupied by the Michel family: the twin gables of Gothic House are outlined as they appeared before the castellated front was added, and other buildings seen in the row are still familiar. The Green is enclosed by a high fence, the gift of George II's wife, Caroline of Anspach, to the Royal manor. This pleased the tenants

EARLY EIGHTEENTH-CENTURY DEVELOPMENT

and they planned to erect Queen Caroline's effigy in the centre of the turf, an idea that remained unfulfilled.

They could have commemorated appropriately the pastrycooks, the Burdekins, whose cheese tartlets, the "Maids of Honour" brought local fame. I find it difficult to believe the traditional story of their origin—that a Maid purloined an old Court recipe and gave it to the pastrycooks, because George III ordered regular supplies of the tartlets to be sent to him. Therefore it is improbable that the Royal cooks knew how to make them with the essential, mysterious Burde-kin flavour. It seems more likely that these Thames Valley culinary geniuses experimented in their humble shop in Hill Street with novel fillings, and having concocted one that delighted the fastidious palate, named it after the new houses on the Green.

Or a statue might have honoured the Widow Boddicott, the pioneer of Richmond's multitudinous tea-shop owners. The Widow organised an Assembly, and in 1738 announced that "Gentlemen and Ladies may have Coffee, Tea or Chocolate any Day of the Week for which constant Attendance will be given."

It is true these fashionable beverages were served at public break-fasts at the Wells, then rising to the full tide of prosperity. They were patronised by all the best people and Pope's

> Sir Plume, of amber snuff-box justly vain,
> And the nice conduct of a clouded cane

aired his best brocade coat as he strolled in the grounds, played cards, danced or amused himself by participating in raffles—the prizes were gold chains, quaint toys, fine china.

The first playhouse was opened on the Hill, above the ferry in 1718; it was built on the site occupied formerly by Scott's Royal Ass-House. One of its early productions, entitled *Richmond Wells*, was lively with local colour for it introduced the "Dog" Inn (later the "Talbot" Hotel facing the Bridge, and now replaced by a cinema); the comedian was rolled down Ferry Hill and the hero rowed the heroine from the Wells. This humble theatre was replaced by another about fifteen years later, chiefly remembered because when it lacked a licence, Theophilus, unsatisfactory son of the Poet Laureate Cibber, ingeniously solved the difficulty. He advertised that he had opened a cephalic snuff warehouse in the "late theatre", adding that the premises were also used to instruct young actors, who gave gratuitous performances.

As pedestrians strolled up the Hill, they saw the tilemakers at work on the slopes of the common or waste land. A tile-kiln had been established there "Time out of Mind", and in 1699, the owners were cautioned for selling tiles made of local clay outside the village, contrary to the custom of the Royal manor. Charges had been made against those who removed clay soil greedily to use in the tile-kiln but the practice had continued. Matthew Moody, Samuel Rundell, Rundell Pigg and Isaac Pigg all in their day, set their underlings to scoop up the clay and subsidences had occurred which had alarmed the residents. (Landslides which have taken place in the Terrace Gardens this century have been attributed to the activities of these old industrialists.) But the tilemakers' days were drawing to an end, and in the mid-eighteenth century, the Court Rolls referred to the "late Tile-Kiln".

In the year 1738, John Christopher opened a humble tavern— the "Star and Garter"—on the Hill summit, for which he paid Lord Dysart the annual rent of forty shillings. There was no accommoda- tion for travellers, but it was an attractive spot and overlooked the sweep of the Thames Valley. Below the green slopes, large barges, some with red sails, drifted along the river. The district had grown into an horticulture centre and these vessels plied to London, laden with colourful pyramids of fruit and vegetables, gilded by the rising sun. Richard Steele described a journey he made from Richmond to London in one of the produce barges: he rose at four in the morning to catch the boat, and was pleased with the simple companions he found on board—the gardeners travelling with their wares to sell in the markets. By the time they arrived at the Strand Bridge, they were accompanied by ten sail of apricot boats.

2

Richmond Lodge passed into history as the house where George II received the news of his Royal sire's death in Hanover. Angry at being awakened from his afternoon siesta, the new king dangled his

27   Richmond: Maids of Honour Row (1724)

28 Richmond: Trumpeter's House, built in the eighteenth century and restored in 1952

breeches in his hand as he shouted to the Prime Minister, Sir Robert Walpole, "Dat is von big lie!"

The Lodge was settled upon Queen Caroline, who made elaborate, expensive alterations in the Gardens. Bridgeman designed bosky woods, romantic wildernesses and serpentine paths. He introduced the sunk ditch, known as the ha-ha, which gave effective boundaries but did not obstruct the view: the device was stated to have originated in France and acquired its name from the surprised exclamation made by those whose walks were checked by its unexpected appearance. Bridgeman's boundaries remain and a long water-filled ha-ha runs from Kew Gardens to the end of the Old Deer Park.

The Queen adorned her Gardens with "fancies", fashionable and quaint little buildings. The most original of these was the absurd Merlin's Cave designed by William Kent. It had Gothic characteristics and its timber and plaster walls were topped by a grotesque thatched roof resembling a tall bee-hive flanked by two smaller ones. Inside the Cave she placed an odd collection of wax figures— "Queen Elizabeth", a "Queen of the Amazons", "Minerva" and a "Witch", grouping them round "Merlin". A local tradesman's wife allowed her features to be copied for the "Witch"; the others were replicas of the faces of the Royal Household.

Merlin's Cave was placed in charge of the Queen's protégé, Stephen Duck, the self-educated thresher poet who began life as a Wiltshire farm boy. His simple verses pleased his Royal patron, but Duck and the "fancy" were the butts of much bitter, well-aimed satire, especially from the pens of Pope and Swift. The public, admitted to the Gardens on certain days, however, were interested in the Cave, and their approval encouraged Caroline to build a second one. This was the Hermitage, prepared to accommodate the busts of ancient and modern philosophers. Its roughly placed stonework enclosed an octagonal room and its miniature bell-topped tower was reached by a winding path. In a poem, entitled "On Richmond Park and Royal Gardens", Duck chanted:

> Or bear me, Nymphs, to the sequester'd Cell,
> Where BOYLE and NEWTON, mighty Sages! dwell;
> Whose Fame shall live, altho' the Grot decay,
> Long as those sacred Truths their Works display.

These by no means completed the Queen's "fancies" and she increased them, delighting in their whimsicalities, until an unwelcome neighbour arrived to jeer. He was her eldest son, Frederick, Prince of Wales, who was on bad terms with his parents. He and his wife, the Princess Augusta of Saxe-Coburg, established a rival Court in Lord Capel's old home, Kew House. The two residences were separated only by the ancient public highway, Love Lane, which can be traced on the 1771 Plan of the Royal Manor, made under the direction of Peter Burrell, the King's Surveyor-General.

Kew House, alluded to sometimes as the White House, and later as Kew Palace(33), had had one of its wings converted into an observatory by Lady Elizabeth Capel's husband, Molyneux, and here Dr. Bradley, later Astronomer-Royal, discovered the aberration of light and the mutation of the earth's axis. In John Evelyn's time the house had been an old timber dwelling, but it had been rebuilt, and the Prince commissioned William Kent to make some alterations to it. Kent also decorated its interior—he painted the ceilings of the drawing-rooms in a lively fashion and gave the gallery a blue and gilt wainscot. He replanned the gardens and the Prince worked in them constantly, compelling his family to plant, dig and weed with him, and, as Budd Dodington lamented, at times he set his friends horticultural tasks.

It was through Dodington's influence that the poet, James Thomson, was drawn within the orbit of the Kew House circle. Thomson detested patronage, but, nevertheless, his life was ameliorated by the financial benefits he received from his acquaintance with Frederick and his friends. *The Masque of Alfred*, with its stirring ode, "Rule Britannia", which he and David Mallet were commissioned to write, was dedicated to the Prince in 1737, the year after the poet settled in Richmond.

Thomson was attracted to Richmond primarily because his friend, Alexander Pope, was charmed with rustic Twickenham. Pope gave the Prince a dog which had an amusing inscription on its collar:

I am his Highness' dog at Kew,
Pray, tell me, sir, whose dog are you?

98

His little, bent figure wrapped in a light greatcoat, Alexander frequently crossed the river to visit James. The latter's first home in Richmond was a humble cottage but the Rates Books show that he moved to a larger one in Kew Foot Lane (now the Kew Foot Road) in 1739. It had seven rooms, and the catalogue of its contents, sold by auction in 1749, after Thomson's death, proved that it was comfortably furnished, with mahogany and walnut pieces and had green damask window curtains.

The poet worked in a summer-house in the garden, where he revised *The Seasons*, wrote plays and *The Castle of Indolence*. He composed long letters to Miss Elizabeth Young, his "Amanda", with whom he sometimes walked in the neighbourhood.

> Which Way, AMANDA, shall we bend our Course?
> The Choice perplexes. Wherefore should we chuse?
> All is the same with Thee. Say, shall we wind
> Along the Streams? or walk the smiling Mead?
> Or court the Forest-Glades? or wander wild
> Among the waving Harvests? or ascend,
> While radiant Summer opens all its Pride,
> Thy Hill, delightful *Shene?*

Thomson was bitterly disappointed when Miss Young refused to marry him. He went more frequently at nights with his friends to the "Castle" or to the "Orange Tree" Taverns. Mrs. Hobart, his housekeeper, was anxious when she saw him set out on these carousals, especially when he was accompanied by the old actor, Quin, who always encouraged the poet to drink more than was good for him. Often the sun had risen on the cherubs on the doorways of those houses near his cottage before he passed them on his way home.

Shortly before his forty-ninth birthday, he developed a cold, contracted on the river—he had hired a boat to take him from Hammersmith to Kew, after he had walked from London to Hammersmith in the heat. He appeared to recover, but a fever followed and a few days later he died. He was buried in the Richmond Parish Church on August 29th, 1748, but it was not until 1792 that he was commemorated by the brass tablet, the gift of the

Earl of Buchan, which he affixed to the wall. It is inscribed with
lines from "Winter":

> Father of Light and Life! Thou good Supreme!
> O teach me what is good! teach me Thyself!
> Save me from folly, vanity, and vice,
> From every low pursuit, and feed my soul
> With knowledge, conscious peace, and virtue pure,
> Sacred, substantial, never-fading bliss!

The sensitive poet, William Collins, who had lodged in Richmond to be near his friend, left the neighbourhood immediately
after Thomson's death and could not be persuaded to return. Mr.
Ragsdale, in whose house Collins stayed, related later how he would
read aloud his odes, then, discouraged, toss them into the fire.

The Royal Hospital in the Kew Foot Road has been built
gradually around the nucleus of Thomson's cottage. George Ross
bought and enlarged it—from his name the word "Rosedale" is
believed to have evolved, for it is often referred to as Rosedale
Cottage. Later it was occupied by the Hon. Frances Boscawen,
who maintained it as a shrine dedicated to the memory of the "sweet
singer of the Seasons". Then the Earl of Shaftesbury acquired the
property and built a mansion around the cottage. After the marriage
of the Prince and Princess of Wales in 1863, the organisers of local
celebrations suggested that their balance of forty pounds should be
used to found a small hospital. Funds augmented and the deceased
Dowager Countess of Shaftesbury's mansion and grounds were
purchased for the purpose.

Traces of those who lived on the site in bygone times have not
been obliterated completely from this unusual hospital. As we
approach its porticoed entrance we see two unusual wrought-iron
lamp-holders, shaped like balls, and quaint metal link extinguishers,
fine examples of Georgian craftsmanship. A room with an elaborate
cornice and a stately staircase date from the Shaftesbury mansion.
Two old garlanded door brackets on a corner wall of a passage overlooking the garden are significant, for they seem to indicate the door
of Thomson's cottage. A clock, framed in a strip of dentilled moulding, preserved from a demolished room, tells the time to patients'

29 Ham Common: Ormeley Lodge. An early eighteenth-century House
with wings added in the early nineteenth century

30 Petersham: Douglas House, built originally in the late seventeenth century
and enlarged in the mid-eighteenth by the Duchess of Queensberry

31 Sudbrook Park, Petersham: The Cube Room (1726-28)

friends as they sit on a bench in the entrance hall, waiting for admission to the wards. Above their heads, a deep arch crosses the
ceiling, indicating where, just over two centuries ago, the wall
divided the poet's bedroom and sitting-room.

4

In ancient days, Sudbrook Park, now occupied by the Richmond
Golf Club, was a hamlet of Petersham. George I leased thirty
acres of Richmond Park to the second Duke of Argyll and Greenwich, who paid an annual rent of six pounds for the land.

The Duke engaged the architect, James Gibbs, to design him a
country home and the two-storied mansion was built between
1726–8(31). Its warm red bricks are relieved on the north and
south sides by four immense Corinthian stone columns which soar
up to the porticoes, almost to the level of the balustraded parapet.
Describing it in his *Book of Architecture*, Gibbs mentions its special
characteristics: "Here is a cube room of 30 feet, handsomely adorn'd
and lighted from two Porticoes. It has two apartments off and over
them lodging-rooms. There are vaults and other offices underground. The house is built of brick except the ornaments which
are of Portland stone." Modern Sudbrook shows a deviation from
this description, for an additional room has been built beneath the
south portico.

The Cube Room is the members' dining-hall. It is panelled in
pine, which, like the rest of the room, has been redecorated recently
in carefully studied shades of cream. Its five heavy oak doors are
flanked by coupled Corinthian pilasters and each pedimented doorway is surmounted by a stucco trophy of arms—plumed helmets,
coats of mail and ancient weapons, their details picked out in gold.
A niche on one wall faces an immense grey marble chimney-piece,
its sculptured lines merging into two classical feminine heads. The
chimney-piece encloses a bevelled mirror, embellished with a
miniature, enamelled, gilt intaglio of the ducal arms. The arms
reappear, carved on a panel above the mirror, the supporting lions,
the boar's head crest and the galleys with pennants flying, emphasised by gold decoration.

The vaulted ceiling sweeps down to an oblong, enclosing the chandelier: and above the cornice are *œil-de-bœuf* windows on one side and roundels on the others. Each window, each roundel is crowned by a decorative scallop shell, in which sits a charming cherub.

A sumptuous room, a poem in marble, woods and stucco, an adequate setting for the second Duke, the great soldier and premier Whig peer. But it is possible that the little Duchess would have preferred a more homely apartment, for she found it difficult to live up to the elegant standards of Sudbrook. In her memoirs of the Argyll family, Lady Louisa Stuart, daughter of George III's Prime Minister, Lord Bute, emphasised the Duchess's characteristics, stressed her habit of chattering continually about trivialities, of clattering with the tea things, of addressing endearing words to her cats and dogs, as she encouraged them to settle in the best chairs.

Before her marriage, the second Duchess of Argyll was Mistress Jenny Warburton, of good Cheshire stock, but with unpolished manners and a certain unrefinement of speech. She was Maid of Honour to Queen Anne, an office she continued to fill under Caroline, Princess of Wales, but she was always in trouble, for she invariably said and did the wrong thing. But then, if she had not made a certain blunder, she would not have become the mistress of Sudbrook Park.

Lady Louisa related the story of the Duke's courtship. It began, one year on Queen Anne's birthday, when Argyll, who seldom went to Court, arrived, resplendent with military glory, to be invested with the Order of the Garter. How handsome he was, how charming his manners—he was the hero of the day. It was customary on that Royal anniversary for the Lord Chamberlain to give a dinner to the Maids of Honour, and, the banquet over, each Maid was called upon in turn to toast a man—any man she fancied. The sophisticated women knew well how to avoid the trap, and named some safe elderly bishop or statesman.

But that night when it was Jenny's turn, she raised her glass and toasted the man who was uppermost in her thoughts—the Duke of Argyll. At this revelation her companions hooted with laughter, and the girl was quizzed so mercilessly about "her conquest", that she burst into tears.

A State ball followed the dinner and the Lord Chamberlain, meeting the Duke there, told him of Jenny's discomfort. Regretful that he had been the cause of her tears, and wishing to make amends, he asked for an introduction to the Maid of Honour. The quizzers noticed that he devoted himself to the plain little Cheshire girl for the rest of the evening; they observed that after that night, he called on her frequently. Soon it was obvious that the Duke was in love with Jenny. His intentions were doubtful, for he had an ailing wife, whom he detested and from whom he lived apart. But Jenny resisted his blandishments and her virtue remained unassailed.

Then suddenly the obstacle was removed, for the Duchess died. Tongues clacked—what would Argyll do now that he was free to wed Jenny? Surely he would never be so foolish as to—but the gossips soon knew, for six months later the pair were married.

The Duke loved the plain, inelegant little woman all his life, although she cramped his style, bored his friends and was guilty of petty meannesses. She failed to give him an heir and was more resentful than he, that their four children were girls. Not wishing to be disturbed by his daughters' chatter, their father built what was termed "The Young Ladies' House", said to be the annexe by the side of the mansion. Meanly educated and left to their own devices, they developed into romps and were nicknamed, "The Screaming Sisterhood", "The Bawling Campbells".

Many original documents relating to properties in Ham and Petersham were lost in air raids in the Second World War, and with them those clues that lead to certainty. Ormeley Lodge (29), which stands on Ham Common, outside the walls of Sudbrook Park, most likely played its part in the story of the second Duke of Argyll's family. The Duke's crest ornaments the handsome entrance gate which, with the railings are attributed to Buncker; the house is con-temporary with Sudbrook Park, its arched windows resemble those of the mansion. Ormeley's main façade—wings were added at a later date—is finished with brick pilasters and a dentilled brick cornice. The doorcase is centred with cherubs set in a frieze of palm-leaves and fruit; the rooms, light, lofty, their decorations restrained, are rich with pine, the staircase walls with oak. A wall niche in the dining-room has a pine hood, a cherub forming the keystone, the spandrels delicate with birds and foliage.

We can visualise the Campbells, as they grew to dignified woman-hood, living in this gracious house. The eldest, Lady Caroline, who inherited Sudbrook after her mother's death and became Baroness Greenwich in her own right, married first the Earl of Dalkeith, then the statesman, Charles Townshend. Another daugh-ter, Lady Betty, wedded James Stuart Mackenzie, whose estate, close to Sudbrook, was inherited by the Bute family. The youngest, Lady Mary, who divorced Lord Coke, spent much time at Sud-brook until her mother's death, and when she lived at Notting Hill she returned continually to Petersham.

Lady Mary kept a detailed journal, written in the form of letters to her sisters, and from this we learn much about eighteenth-century Petersham, Richmond and Kew. One Sunday, for example, she saw four peeresses, and three of them duchesses, in Petersham Church. She enjoyed her visits to the Duchess of Montrose in winter-time, because the Duchess kept up good fires and she found the "great room" at Sudbrook cold. She mentioned Mr. Ord, Baron of the Exchequer of Scotland, who married Sir John Darnall's daughter, and who lived in a house on the site of the present Petersham Lodge. But the Petersham Lodge visited by Lady Mary, was the mansion Burlington designed for Lord Harrington, who was created an earl in 1742, his heir taking the courtesy title of Lord Petersham. His was the third home to be built on the spot: first, there had been the Cole manor-house, surrendered to Charles I, when he enclosed the New Park. This was replaced by Lord Rochester's Petersham Lodge, destroyed by fire in 1721. The site was unlucky for Harrington's mansion was demolished in the nineteenth century by the Com-missioners of Woods and Forests and the grounds, indicated now only by great cedar trees, were converted into Petersham Park.

Lady Mary referred frequently in her journal to Lord Rochester's daughter, Matthew Prior's, "lovely Kitty", the Duchess of Queens-berry. The Duchess had inherited Lord Carleton's mansion, later called Douglas House after Archibald, Lord Douglas, husband of Lady Frances Scott.

Lying at the end of a drive, a few yards from the picturesque Gatehouse of Ham House and facing Petersham Walk, Douglas House has a characteristic late Stuart steep, hipped roof over a pedimented gable(30). To the main block, distinctive with its fine red brickwork, the Duchess, in 1766, added a north wing in brown bricks, and she was responsible for its unusual planning. Lady Mary, who always stressed the Duchess's eccentricities, thought her idea of architectural design, "very whimsical"; while one ground-floor room was 30 feet long and 11 feet high, the adjoining apartment was the same length but only 7 feet high. The first of these rooms, the drawing-room, has survived, but there are no odd, fantastic ceilings to be seen today in this splendid house.

In the Duchess's day, a banqueting-hall stood in the grounds, its roof a landmark from Richmond Hill. This has vanished but its foundations, concealed by a little coppice, reveal a deep ice-cellar where ice, gathered from the frozen ponds in winter was preserved for use at summer fêtes. A lead cistern embossed with the Queensberry arms, ornaments the rock garden.

Doubtless the Duchess would have been charmed by a modern innovation in the grounds—a swimming-pool, a dressing-room at its side camouflaged to resemble an old tiled barn. Some of the tall trees on the lawn had been planted when rehearsals of *The Beggar's Opera* were held in the garden. John Gay sheltered under the Duchess's influential wing; her championship of the opera's banned sequel *Polly*, resulted in a Royal request that she should absent herself from Court.

"A spoilt, wistful beauty, most bewitching, most perverse, most provoking, with superior natural parts and what the Scotch call 'an enormous bee in her bonnet'." This was Lady Louisa Stuart's description of Her Grace, who was the secret delight of the Twickenham intellectuals. Pope praised her beauty, but disparaged her intellect, and Horace Walpole, newly settled in his Gothic "castle", Strawberry Hill, wrote, "Thank God, the Thames is between me and the Duchess of Queensberry." They waited expectantly, anticipating her next sensational move, her latest witticism. She refused to follow fashion but dressed in the outmoded styles of her youth: she upset local conventions by sweeping into social gatherings at the hour when it was customary for them to break up, and once, when she visited Sudbrook Park, the guests were resentful because she rearranged their chairs in less formal fashion.

Her best and truest friend in the neighbourhood, the Countess of Suffolk, lived across the river at Marble Hill, the house designed by Lord Burlington and Lord Pembroke, its garden laid out by Pope and Lord Bathurst.

Petersham became the home of another, but totally different celebrity, before the eighteenth century closed. In May 1798, an important, but at the time, little heeded entry was made in the Parish Registers; it recorded the burial of Captain George Vancouver of the Royal Navy, the explorer who discovered the island which was named after him. Every year, in modern times, the anniversary of his death is commemorated by Canadians, who, with their English friends, gather around Vancouver's grave in Petersham churchyard, and a simple service is conducted by the Vicar, the Rev. R. S. Mills. Friendly links are maintained between the city of Vancouver and Petersham.

After he returned to England in 1795, Vancouver, requested by the Admiralty to write an account of his last voyage, settled in the village, from which during subsequent years, he headed his corre-spondence. Sometimes he stayed at the already famous "Star and Garter" Hotel on Richmond Hill and the landlady's daughter stoutly maintained that, as he looked from one of its windows, she heard him exclaim, "In all my travels, I never clept eyes on a more beautiful spot than this. Here would I live and here would I die."

But where were his lodgings? That is the question many Canad-ians ask, when they go to the village, anxious to retrace his footsteps. They are directed to walk along River Lane, past Petersham Lodge, past the Manor House, worth noting as a good example of Georgian architecture, its interesting doorcase revealed at the end of its long front garden. Then the pilgrims come to a white cottage with a quaint, irregular tiled roof—The Glen. This, according to local tradition, supported by research, was Vancouver's last home, where, charts, journals and astrolabe at hand, he wrote *Voyage of Discovery*.

5

Eighteenth-century Richmond had its local hero, its village Hampden—John Lewis, brewer, who won the Battle of Richmond Park. His portrait, painted when he was an old man, by Reynolds's pupil, T. Stewart, hangs in the Richmond Public Library. His determined chin sinks into his kerchief, a low, broad hat covers his abundant hair, he wears a plain dark suit and holds a long staff. Engravings of this portrait were given honoured places in many local homes, for as the Rev. Thomas Wakefield (Minister of the Parish Church from 1776 to 1804) stated in the inscription he wrote to accompany the portrait, Lewis recovered the people's right to a free passage through the Park, of which they had been robbed.

In the early eighteenth century, Queen Anne's cousin, Henry Hyde, Earl of Clarendon was the Park Ranger, but the office was coveted by Sir Robert Walpole, who persuaded George II to give it to his son, Robert Walpole junior. Clarendon sold the remainder of his term to the King for five thousand pounds. The Prime Minister, who kept a pack of beagles in the Park, spent his week-ends there and the closing of the House of Commons on Saturdays, dates from this period. Walpole rebuilt a Stuart farmhouse, Harleton Lodge, once owned by the Coles of Petersham, as his Park residence and called it Old Lodge. It was pulled down in the nineteenth century.

Nominally the son was Ranger, but Walpole ruled the Park. He spent thousands of pounds on the construction of his house and on improvements to the enclosed acres, which he said the Hydes had neglected. Then, on the pretext that the Park was infested with poachers and that the public interfered with the hunting, he curtailed the people's privileges, given to them by Charles I. He removed the ladder-stiles from the walls, built lodges at the gates, and ordered the keepers to admit only "respectable people" and such carriages as had passes. These passes were obtained easily and the new regulations did not cause inconvenience to local residents.

The Hanoverian Royal family welcomed Richmond Park as one of the best-stocked hunting grounds in England. "On Saturday their Majesties", reported the *Stamford Mercury* in August 1728, "together with their Royal Highnesses the Duke (of Cumberland) and the Princesses, came to the new park by Richmond from Hamp- ton Court and diverted themselves with hunting a stag, which ran from eleven to one, when he took to the great pond, where he de- fended himself for half an hour, when he was killed. His Majesty, the Duke, and the Princess Royal hunted on horseback, her Majesty and the Princess Amelia in a four-wheeled chaise, Princess Caroline in a two-wheeled chaise, and the Princesses Mary and Louisa in a coach. Her Majesty was pleased to show great condescension and com- plaisance to the country people by conversing with them, and order- ing them money. Several of the nobility attended, amongst them Sir Robert Walpole, clothed in green as Ranger. When the diversion was over their Majesties, the Duke, and the Princesses refreshed themselves on the spot with a cold collation, as did the nobility at some distance of time after, and soon after two in the afternoon returned to Hampton Court."

George II kept flocks of wild turkeys in the Park, and the hapless birds, chased by dogs, were forced up trees, so that the King could take easy aim. This sporting monarch commissioned Lord Pembroke to design him a shooting-box in this favourite rural retreat and the main block of White Lodge, built of Portland stone, was begun in 1727. At first it was called Stone Lodge, then it became New Lodge to distinguish it from Walpole's house.

The new building was appreciated by Queen Caroline and the avenue by which it was approached from the Richmond gate, was named "The Queen's Ride" in her honour. Sir Walter Scott gave an elaborate description of the Park's scenic beauty in *The Heart of Midlothian*, for it was in this avenue that his heroine, Jennie Deans, pleaded with Caroline for the life of her sister Effie. The Queen had a private road cut from Richmond Lodge to the Park, and its route can be traced on Rocque's map of 1745. Prime Minister Walpole spent some unhappy half-hours negotiating for this road with Sarah, Duchess of Marlborough, for it had to be carried through the manor of Wimbledon, of which she was the owner. The Duchess, angered by Caroline's tactless remarks, uttered publicly about the deceased Duke, refused the concession. But the Queen insisted that she must have her road. Walpole finally persuaded the Duchess to give

32 "The Palace at Kew": Kew House, sometimes called the White House

From an eighteenth-century print

33 Ormonde Lodge (1704), later known as Richmond Lodge

Reproduced by Gracious Permission of H.M. The Queen from the painting by Thomas Sandby

34 Kew Palace, also known as the Dutch House (1631)

way and the Queen agreed to pay £300 to be distributed to the poor of Wimbledon who used the common land through which the new road was cut.

Robert Walpole junior died in 1751 and George II appointed his daughter, Princess Amelia, as Ranger. More autocratic than Charles I, she insisted that the Park was her private domain, excluded the public completely, and admitted only her family and a few friends. Petitions the tactless Princess refused to consider were published in contemporary newspapers; protest meetings were held and eventually a group of influential residents brought a lawsuit against the Deputy Ranger to establish their rights to a carriage road. The trial was a farce, the action was lost and East Sheen residents subscribed over £1000 to pay the costs. Amelia, jubilant, had won the first round of the fight.

John Lewis, the brewer, who had followed the trial closely, believed that the battle could be reopened—this time the case could be based on the people's ancient right to a footway through the Park. He staged a scene—he tried to follow a carriage through the East Sheen Gate, allowed the woman keeper to push him out and brought his action. His suit was heard at the Kingston Assizes on April 3rd, 1758, before Sir Michael Foster, King's Bench Judge. The verdict was in Lewis's favour; democracy had been vindicated and Richmond Park was opened once more to the people.

In the following month ladder-stiles were placed again at the East Sheen and Ham Gates. May 16th was a day of jubilation. Villagers came from miles around and shouted and sang as they swarmed into Amelia's paradise. But there was a sharp sting to the victory; the ladder-steps had been erected spitefully and were placed so far apart that old men and children could not climb them. Lewis, furious at this injustice, waited until Foster was again at the Kingston Assizes and then complained about the manner in which the Judge's instructions had been carried out. He was asked to see that the steps were constructed so that not only old men and children, but that old women, too, could use them.

At the time of the trial the brewer was a well-to-do man, but his last years were clouded by poverty: he had business reverses and his anxieties were increased by a flood tide which burst open the doors of his brewery in the Petersham Road and washed away his papers. His neighbours, always grateful that he had effected the reopening of Richmond Park, subscribed to provide him with an annuity of fifty pounds, and shortly before his death in 1792, when he was seventy-nine years of age, the well-known actress, Mrs. Jordan gave a benefit performance for him.

As soon as Princess Amelia heard the result of Lewis's lawsuit, she declared that the downfall of England had begun with the opening of Richmond Park and she resigned the Rangership. While she held this appointment she resided occasionally at White Lodge (45, 46) and indeed, was the first person to live there. She commis-sioned Robert Morris to design the two brick wings we see there today, but although the work was begun, it remained unfinished for some years. Lady Mary Coke visited this Royal residence in 1766 and described its interior thus: ". . . the chief curiosity is an Indian paper in the Great room which cost three guineas the sheet; it looks like japan but being on a dark ground makes the room appear dismal: the chimney-pieces are I think very paltry. The King and Queen has drank tea there every Sunday evening all the summer."

6

You will find the *Sophora japonica* on the verge of a path winding from the Broad Walk in Kew Gardens. It looks like an old man doubled up with lumbago—so bent is its trunk—and it is supported by crutches. This is not surprising, for 200 years have passed since, introduced by William Gordon of Mile End, it came to England. It was one of the first specimens from overseas to reach the Botanic Gardens, and it arrived only two years after the death in 1751 of Frederick, Prince of Wales. It had been there six years when the future George III, educated in the Dutch House, Kew, attained the age of twenty-one. That June 4th was a great day in the hamlet, for it was celebrated by the opening of the first bridge to span the Thames between Kew and Brentford. And what a curious con-struction it was, its large, centre wooden arches sloping like a switch-back! It was the private property of Robert Tunstall, owner of the horse-ferry who believed the tolls would be remunerative. Certainly he must have congratulated himself at the end of the first day, for 3000 people, attracted by the novelty, crossed it. One hundred workmen who had built it were given a dinner and that night Kew blazed with a bonfire and illuminations. From that time the Green, regarded previously as "waste", was railed and the Prince offered to provide a road through it to the Bridge.

The *Sophora japonica* saw interesting things happening inside the Gardens at this period. We may be certain that this foreigner from China, was noticed by young William Chambers, who was prospecting the landscape with a professional eye. Anything that reminded the architect of his travels in the Far East, attracted him, and who knows but the *Sophora japonica* inspired the Pagoda, begun in the autumn of 1761?

The Kew Gardens Pagoda (35) was not, as many people imagine, brought in pre-fabricated sections from the Far East. In his folio volume, *Plan of Gardens and Buildings at Kew*, Chambers described how it took six months to erect. It is 163 feet high and is divided into ten storeys: the lowest of these is 26 feet in diameter and 18 feet high, and there is a decrease of 1 foot in diameter and height respectively with each successive storey. A year later he was proud to find that, despite its height, neither crack nor fracture had appeared. It was unaffected by German bombs which exploded near the site in 1941.

It must have been a scintillating sight when it was finished, different from the somewhat sedate aspect it presents today. Its projecting roofs glittered like rainbows, for they were covered with varnished iron plates of different colours, and at their angles eighty dragons crouched, each dragon enclosed by thin, tinted glass which produced a dazzling reflection. The top ornament was double-gilt. Some of Chambers' ornamental buildings at Kew, such as the Moorish Alhambra, the Theatre of Augusta, and the House of Confucius, have vanished. One of his classical "fancies", the Temple of the Sun, perished only in 1916, during a storm when a cedar crashed upon its fragility. It stood in the centre of the Dowager Princess of Wales' Botanic Garden and its site is marked by a maidenhair tree, planted by Queen Mary, not far from its stately ancestor, the Princess Augusta's maidenhair tree, now about 80 feet.

decorated with figures and trophies and other extreme embellishments from which on each side was a range of statues, supporting festoons of flowers in proper colours: at the termination on each side were two lesser arches through which appeared emblematical pictures alluding to the arts and sciences, the whole in extent 200 feet. These were all transparencies with such outside illuminations as the design would admit. The great arch led into a very superb enclosed pavilion in the centre of which was a dome supported by eight columns wreathed with flowers and ornamented with gold: from the centre the plan extended four ways, with apartments within for a band of music, sideboards and the whole decorated with paintings."

Richmond Lodge grew too small for the rapidly increasing Royal family, and George III decided to build a new residence. Mrs. Papendiek, whose father was a Royal Page, stated in her memoirs (*Court and Private Life in the Time of Queen Charlotte*), how in the autumn of 1769, the King "was greatly occupied in digesting plans with Sir William Chambers for a new palace at Richmond". It was to have an uninterrupted view of the river, of the Hill, Cholmondeley Walk and part of the Green. "It was begun. To make it complete for the prospect I have endeavoured to point out, and for other purposes of elegance and convenience, a small piece of ground was necessary that was not in the Royal manor, and therefore must be purchased from the authorities of the town. This they refused. The building nevertheless went on as far as the ground floor but then was stopped, and then their Majesties determined to move to Kew."

"The King", wrote Lady Mary Coke in August 1770, "has laid the foundations for a Lodge (alas! not a palace) in Richmond Gardens, very near where the old now stands: 'tis to be 140 feet and to be built on arches as I suppose to command a greater prospect."

The new residence must have been planned close to the Royal Observatory, which, designed by Chambers, and built of Portland stone, with a movable dome, was ready for the King to watch the transit of Venus in 1769. The Observatory occupied the approximate site of the former Carthusian monastery and the Priory Gate was removed only in 1770, when George III, possibly with a view to extending the gardens of his prospective home, ordered the entire hamlet of West Sheen to be obliterated. A plan of this land was

drawn up in 1754 when the Surveyor-General noted that the buildings on the monastery site were in a bad condition. One of the
tenants was a Mr. Andrews, a calico printer—this industry had been
carried on here since the late Stuart period, and near his building was
the field marked "Bleaching Ground". The acres where the hamlet
had stood were turned by the King into pasture ground, used for his
livestock—Farmer George had purchased a large farm in the neighbourhood—and today they are part of the Old Deer Park.

Stephen Demainbray (he lived at No. 22, Richmond Green) was
the first Royal Observer: the Observatory was used as an educational
centre by the princes, and as has been proved by the discovery of
certain tools, the King established his own workshop there.

Kew Observatory, as it is now known, lies beyond the Royal
Mid-Surrey Golf Club, and almost faces Syon House across the
river. Chambers' building remains much as he designed it, although
wings have been added. Rusticated stonework rises above the
mound on which it stands, and steps lead to lofty, connecting,
octagonal rooms. The walls of each room are lined with immense
cupboards, closed by sheets of rare Georgian curved glass, decorated
with strapwork. The obelisks in the Old Deer Park are a souvenir
of the days when the Observatory gave London its official time.

The building has known many vicissitudes. Nowadays it is
administered by the Meteorological Office, and is the centre of many
interesting scientific experiments. To the public it is known best as
the place which gives weather guidance. Some of the apparatus is
arranged on the tranquil lawns outside the Observatory. When the
weather is unusually dry, the scientists can see the foundations of the
Carthusian monastery at their feet, outlined clearly on the grass,
haunting reminder of the site's former occupants.

Chapter VIII

GEORGIAN PROMENADE

George III and Queen Charlotte—Asgill House—The Highwaymen—The Misses Houblon—The Terrace—Houses on The Hill—Two Acts of Parliament—Theatre Royal—Richmond Bridge—William Cobbett—Kew Green Celebrities—Second Kew Bridge—The Dutch House—Horace Walpole—Duke of Queensberry—Duke of Clarence and Mrs. Jordan—Viscount Fitzwilliam—French Émigrés

I

RICHMOND residents, who were old in the early nineteenth century, recalled how, as children, they had often seen George III strolling informally through the streets. Queen Charlotte, Lady of the Royal manor, sometimes accompanied him, a habit of which Lady Mary Coke disapproved. She wrote, "I am not satis-fied in my own mind about the Queen walking in a town un-attended", and there was a disturbance on one such occasion when a crazy woman threw a shoe at Her Majesty. The King always responded to the townsmen's salutations by saying, "Good-morning, friend", and sometimes he stopped to pat the youngsters' cheeks.

In May 1769, Great Street, or High Street, as it was sometimes referred to at the time, was named officially George Street after the Sovereign. Magpye Lane—the "Magpye" Tavern stood next to the Charity School—resumed its historic title, Brewers Lane. Furbelow Street, as the ancient way to the Palace had become known, was changed to King Street. At this period it was Richmond's principal shopping centre and some of the old red-tiled roofs we see there, date from the days when sedan-chairs stopped outside the shops.

In a "Letter to a Society Gentleman", published in a contemporary journal about 1750, a correspondent mentioned an interesting tree he had seen at the junction of Furbelow Street and Great Street. It was "call'd the Stocks Tree from having the stocks near it, said to have been planted by Queen Elizabeth". In 1745 the Court Rolls mentioned, "The Queen's Head near the Stocks Tree."

35　The Pagoda, 1761-62

Sir William Chambers, Architect

36　The Temple of Aeolus, 1761-62, on the Mount

Sir William Chambers, Architect

KEW GARDENS

37　St. Anne's Church

38　Houses of the eighteenth and early nineteenth century on the North Side

KEW GREEN

The stocks themselves had been moved to the site of the ducking-stool by the Town Pond: the latter was reported to be in a bad state in 1759 and the townspeople were threatened with penalties if they had not cleaned it out by the Feast of St. Michael the Archangel. In Burrell's Plan of 1771, the site is marked "The late Town Pond."

The King subscribed to the new organ in the Parish Church, the installation of which was celebrated in 1770 by a concert. A performance of "a sacred Oratorio call'd *Messiah*" was advertised (Lady Mary Coke had a ticket but did not think she would use it). He patronised the cricket matches on the Green, which became fashionable events. We find the "Crickett-Players" Tavern—now the "Cricketers"—mentioned in the Court Rolls in 1770, but once, when Brentford men played a local team, the Royal spectator ordered a dinner for the cricketers at the "Feathers", and tipped both winners and losers handsomely.

Oak House, overlooking the Green at the end of King Street, has retained a delightful souvenir of young George III and Queen Charlotte. Their profiles, crowned and inset in medallions, decorate a splendid moulded ceiling in a first-floor room. These portraits appear in the spandrels of an exquisitely festooned circle, outspread like a delicate white lace web. The house itself, like its neighbour, Old Palace Place, is of late seventeenth-century origin and its ground-floor dining-room is panelled with oak. A panel near the fireplace opens and reveals a cupboard with curved shelves; the inner side is designed with octagons (40, 44).

But much of the house has characteristics of a later period. The staircase, its mahogany handrail poised on slender wrought-iron balustrades, the ornate doorcases and decorations in the first-floor rooms are recognised as the work of a master hand. Sir William Chambers and Sir Robert Taylor have been suggested as possible alternative architects, for both were working in the neighbourhood at the time these additions suggest. Chambers was at Kew and Taylor designed the riverside mansion on the north-west corner of the Old Palace site for Sir Charles Asgill, a former Lord Mayor of London.

To approach Asgill House from Oak House, we cross the Green and go down Old Palace Lane, the ancient way concerning which Sir Gregory Norton quarrelled with his tenants. Before the road was made, it was studded with posts and chains, some of which now encircle the grass plot in Old Palace Yard.

On the left-hand side of the Lane we pass Asgill Lodge, a typical eighteenth-century building, but like many houses in this part of Richmond, partly deceptive, for its front rooms were added to much older premises. And here, on this site once occupied by Royal Tudor domestic offices, we find a fascinating relic of the past in the cellar. This is an ancient, rugged stone table, built against the walls and looking as if it had been there "Time out of Mind". Some of its markings suggest that in bygone centuries it may have been associated with minting. The well in the cellar is now blocked up, like the trap-door in the floor immediately above it.

The wall of Asgill House is a boundary of the former Royal ten acres, a fact to which bypassers' attention is drawn by a stone tablet which records that here stood Henry I's dwelling in 1125, and that three monarchs, Edward III, Henry VII and Elizabeth I, died within the precincts.

Asgill House (12, 43) can be seen best from the towing-path which, incidentally, did not exist in Sir Charles's time for he paid ten shillings a year to use the strip of ground to the river. The mansion rises majestically from a mound, its pale stone fabric gleaming like ivory among the tall trees. A plate in Volume IV of *Vetruvius Britannicus* shows how it appeared when it was first built, before the roof was raised. A stone band, like a sash, interspersed with balustrades divides the first-floor windows from the ground floor, where tall, semicircular leaded casements are set in a rusticated arch. The keystone forms a classical head, probably a representation of Old Father Thames.

The octagonal reception rooms on the ground floor are connected by mirrored panelled doors which reflect the muted colourings of the elaborate decorations. The superb staircase rises in long serpentine flights and a first-floor bedroom, adorned by Andrea Casali, has painted wall panels. Classical divinities—goddesses emerging from pastel-hued clouds—are enclosed by scrolled gilt frames.

Sir Charles's Crown lease for fifty years was signed in October 1762. The land had been rented previously to Moses Hart, a banker, and there were stables and a brewhouse by the river. These are indicated clearly on a plan of the Old Palace site, dated 1754. Possibly Hart, who lived on the other side of the river, intended to build a house here for his daughter, Mrs. Judith Levi. He died in 1756 and Mrs. Levi almost immediately occupied No. 4, Maids of Honour Row.

The previous ownership of the site is of interest because it was a local tradition that the unusual octagonal motif of Asgill House, far more pronounced before the roof was raised, was due to the fact that it had been built on the foundations of an Old Palace turret. Cer-tainly its deep cellars follow the plan, but no sign of such a relic appears in delineations of the Royal site. All we see in the engraving illustrating Grove's *Life and Times of Cardinal Wolsey* (1742) is the low building by the river.

Asgill House's delightful old-world garden extends parallel with the river as far as the Gothic summer-house at the end of Trumpeter's House grounds. The tall copper-beech that shines like molten bronze in the summer, was planted in 1813 by Mrs. Palmer to com-memorate the birth of her grandson. In this garden Asgill entertained City Companies who came up the Thames in their stately barges.

Gay, hospitable days until the American War of Independence cast a shadow across this family, took to the rebellious colonies, the adored son and heir, the young soldier, Captain Charles Asgill. Startling news reached the agonised parents—they heard that their boy, a prisoner of war, was to be shot, a reprisal demanded by General Washington. It was a drama of an "eye for an eye", linked to the hanging of a privateer, Jack Huddy, by the British Forces. Young Asgill's fate was determined by the drawing of lots and he seemed doomed to perish. The father was ill, the mother wore mourning, the little sisters laughed no longer, and then suddenly, just before Christmas 1782, the gloom was lifted from the enchanting octagonal rooms. Charles arrived home, his life saved by the gracious intervention of Louis XVI and Marie Antoinette of France.

An incident that happened one night during a concert held at Sir Charles Asgill's house was mentioned by his neighbour, Lady Cowper, who lived at Cholmondeley House. Writing to her god-daughter, Mary Dewes (Mrs. Delany's niece), she told her how, "An awkward person sat himself down upon a marble sideboard and brought it down with a branch of candles and I desired to know his name that I might never invite him to my house." In September 1769, she described an assembly she gave at Cholmondeley House; her great room was illuminated by more than five dozen waxlights. She had invited sixty guests but only forty arrived: some were sick, others, although she had fixed the date of her *soirée* when the moon was full, were "afraid of being robbed".

This phrase alluded to the highwaymen, the local Macheaths, who congregated in the "Red Cow" Tavern (nicknamed "The Thieves' Kitchen" at the time) in Marsh Gate. They were the terror of the neighbourhood, and social gatherings ended on a note of tension as guests thought of the drive home along dark roads where masked, armed horsemen pounced from behind trees, stopped coaches, and guineas and jewels exchanged hands.

In her letters to Mary, Lady Cowper mentioned many of the social functions she attended in Richmond, but she did not allude to the Wells. For the Assembly Rooms were closed. They became unfashionable and in a last effort to make them pay, prices were lowered and they were patronised by London's rowdiest elements. Their nightly revels were so disturbing that the wealthy Misses Houblon, sober daughters of a deceased Bank of England Governor, enjoyed the luxury of leasing the Wells and closing the entertainment centres.

Rebecca and Susanna Houblon lived in a red-brick house on Richmond Hill—now the premises of the Old Vicarage School— which was occupied subsequently by Mrs. B. A. Ellerker and given Gothic characteristics. In 1757 the sisters founded the nine alms-houses for spinsters which bear their name. Shut off from Worple Way by an imposing iron gate, these buildings have remained unchanged, but the Trustees of the Richmond Charities have modernised them with some pleasant amenities.

The elder Miss Houblon died before she could complete her work, but Susanna fulfilled her wishes and provided nobly for the spinsters. Much of the land which lay between the almshouses and their homes was their own, and after their day, the trustees augmented the almshouses' revenue by studding one of the lanes with small brown houses—the Houblon Road.

2

When Susanna, surviving Houblon sister, died in 1765, she bequeathed the house on the Hill to a relative, stipulating that her niece, Esther Mytton, should be allowed to retain her room there and that no building should be erected which would interfere with the prospect from her windows. It was Mistress Mytton's lot to enjoy the celebrated view in armchair comfort: others, less fortunately situated found the Queen's Terrace (the Terrace) an admirable promenade for landscape gazing, although its rough surface was unkind to delicate shoes.

It was laid out in 1775, the year that The Wick (39), planned by the architect, Robert Mylne, was built at the end of the Terrace for Dame Elizabeth St. Aubyn. The Dame leased the land from the Hickey trustees and before she could build, had first to demolish the old tavern, the "Bull's Head". The Wick was erected at a greater distance from the road than the tavern had been situated.

If we study an old print of this charming house, we see that at first, high walls hid its ground-floor windows, meeting in the admirably proportioned portico. The back of the house is mainly bow-shaped and the reception-rooms here are oval. The interior has an atmosphere of classical elegance, and the walls of the drawing-room, now decorated in pale grey, are ornamented with carved garlands of flowers and fruit, festooned around mirrors. From the windows we see a long terrace garden, at the end of which is an eighteenth-century summer-house with Tuscan columns.

The steep track called Nightingale Lane runs between The Wick and the Terrace meadows. A single cottage once stood here which later evolved into the mansion of the Ladies Ashburnham. This, in its turn, developed into an hotel in the nineteenth century, its balconies and striped, cone-shaped roof reminiscent of a Central European *pension*.

At the foot of Nightingale Lane, just beyond the Terrace meadows, stood the Duke of Montagu's house, its lawns sloping to the Thames. In 1768 the Duchess was granted permission to incorporate into her estate some of the land undermined by the owners of the "late Tile-Kiln". In the following year, Lady Mary Coke, who visited the Duchess, wrote in her journal: "The gardens they are making upon the Hill will be very pretty but it is extremely expensive as all the ground is supported by timber and two sorts of soil are brought to lay over the natural one which is clay." About the same time she related how "Mademoiselle", the Duchess of Buccleuch's dog, had "dyed raving mad", after having bitten the Duchess of Montagu's dog and added quaintly: "'Tis dreadful the number of people who are bit in Richmond; they are all sent to the sea, but 'tis not always effective."

The Duchess of Montagu had an unusual butler, an African negro, Ignatius Sancho, who was born on a slave-ship and brought to England in infancy. Finding that the two maiden ladies who had adopted him, were not educating him, the Duke, who thought him intelligent, lent him books. Sancho wrote a book on the theory of music and his correspondence with contemporary celebrities, published in a volume for which Bartolozzi engraved his portrait, included many letters headed "Richmond".

The Wick almost faces the first house overlooking the Terrace—Doughty House, occupied for many years by a Miss Doughty, who was there in 1786. Later it became the home of Sir Francis Cook, who added a gallery for his noted picture collection. Doughty House replaced an earlier mansion on the site, built by Sir William Richardson, who appears to have lived there from 1744 to 1769, when it was destroyed by fire. Sir William's godson, William Richardson, married Anne, daughter of Christopher Blanchard, the successful maker of playing-cards, and owner of No. 3, the Terrace. Blanchard was admitted as a tenant of the Royal manor in 1768, and the next year—the year he died—according to the Richmond Rates Books, his house was being rebuilt. It is probable that it, too, was affected by the fire.

There is a marked similarity between No. 3, the Terrace and Ely House, Dover Street, London, of which Robert Taylor was the architect in 1772. Looking at a photograph of the London house, Richmond people, at first sight, might well think that this is the familiar building on the Hill. Then they note the differences—No. 3, the Terrace terminates with a pediment, not a stone balus-trade; the original first-floor windows have been exchanged for

French ones; the rusticated stonework is surmounted by a scrolled frieze.

Inside the house, the stairs are stone, the handrail ebonised mahogany, the balustrade of fine wrought iron. The staircase walls are inset with oval plaques, enclosing blue cameo portraits on a cream ground—we wonder, can one of these attractive young women with charming coiffures be a study of Anne Richardson, *née* Blanchard, who inherited the lovely house?

No. 3, the Terrace is not large but its interior decorations are lavish, as if the planner had aimed at creating on Richmond Hill a model, expressing the comprehensive architectural refinements of the period (42). Wherever the eye turns it meets superb detail— decorated ceiling, carved dado, elaborate doorcase, Adam-style mantelpiece. Some attractive stories have been told about the house. It is said that when George III was told that it had been built by his card-maker, he remarked wittily that "all his cards must have turned up trumps". The fragrance of Mrs. Fitzherbert's gracious personality lingers over it, for it has been stated repeatedly that she lived in this house at the dawn of her romance with the future George IV. (Mrs. Fitzherbert's ghost flits gently about the neighbourhood: it has been said that probably she and the Prince of Wales spent their honeymoon at Ormeley Lodge, Ham Common, but her only proved residence in the locality is Marble Hill, Twickenham.) Incidentally, the attempt to fasten the popular ballad "The Lass of Richmond Hill" on to Mrs. Fitzherbert, on account of the line, "I'd crowns resign to call her mine", has failed: undoubtedly it was inspired by a Miss I'Anson of Richmond, Yorkshire. And, as one of George IV's biographers pointed out, the lady was hardly a lass at the time, being twenty-eight and twice married.

Sir William Chambers designed Wick House, neighbour to The Wick, for Sir Joshua Reynolds, who believed that its site stood entirely within the manor of Petersham. He was not absolutely accurate for the vaults of his new home projected into Richmond. He was pulled up sharply in 1772, and told that "he hath encroached therein to the damage of the Lady" (Queen Charlotte was the Lady of the Royal manor), but he was granted leave to extend his vaults for which he paid the annual rent of one shilling.

Miss Palmer, Reynolds's niece, did not like this house perched on the Hill slope, and she complained that it lacked privacy and a good garden. The artist seldom slept there but used it to entertain his friends—Boswell, Hannah More and Fanny Burney referred to these pleasant parties. Fox declared that Reynolds "never enjoyed Richmond since the human face was his landscape", but, nevertheless, the artist painted his famous view of the Petersham and Twickenham meadows from the windows of Wick House.

After his death, his old home lost its original appearance for a subsequent owner encased it in stucco, but recently it has been restored as an annexe for the staff of the Star and Garter Home for Disabled Sailors, Soldiers and Airmen and has resumed its primary character.

George III was always pleased when he met Reynolds on Richmond Hill. The King frequently visited his friend, Sir Lionel Darell at Ancaster House by the Park Gate—his gift to the baronet, sometime a director of the East India Company. Originally a shooting-box had stood there, owned by Peregrine, Duke of Ancaster, but the Darell home which we see today, is a solid, brown brick, bow-winged mansion. Once, when Sir Lionel complained that he had not enough land at the back to build a conservatory the good-natured monarch went into the Park, traced a line with his stick, and presented his friend with the desired ground, for which he paid a small annual rent.

Ancaster House had delightful violet glass windows which, on a fine, frosty morning, gleamed like diamond-set amethysts. Alas! during the Second World War there was an air fight over the Park . . . in a few minutes the ground was covered with shattered glass and the amethysts shone no more on Richmond Hill. It was occupied in 1924 by the late Group Captain Sir Louis Greig and then became an annexe of the Star and Garter Home.

Horace Walpole nicknamed the family at Ancaster Lodge, the "Dancing Darells", because they held weekly balls and his friend, the wit, George Selwyn, groaned about these tame entertainments. In 1795, *The Times* reporting a possible visit of the future George IV to Ancaster House, stated that the Prince thought the baronet "had the best cook in Christendom".

39　The Wick, Richmond Hill (1775)
Robert Mylne, Architect

40　Oak House, Richmond
(late seventeenth century, with
mid-eighteenth century additions)

41　Asgill House, Richmond, (1758)
Sir Robert Taylor, Architect

42　No. 3 The Ter-
race, Richmond Hill
(c. 1769)

43   Asgill House: The Landing
Sir Robert Taylor, Architect

44   Oak House: A detail of the Plaster Ceiling
showing a Medallion of George III

Sir Lionel's daughter, Amelia, was a beauty in the days when she tripped round the ballroom of Ancaster House. Her father died in 1804 and she refused to allow anyone to enter the room he had occupied—it was only after her own decease at a ripe age in the mid-nineteenth century that the door was opened and disclosed that everything was just as the baronet had left it. His cocked hat lay on the table by an unfolded copy of *The Times*.

As she grew old, the once lovely Amelia Darell took her place among Richmond's eccentrics. She collected unconsidered trifles from the streets, odds and ends that were then known as "dress-maker's sweepings". A resident who knew her, recorded that as she neared her end, almost with her last breath, "she betrayed her ruling passion", and asked how many potatoes the servants were cooking.

3

In the year 1768, two gorgeously attired officials appeared in Richmond's streets. Their brown surtout coats were trimmed with scarlet and gold lace and there was gold lace on their hats. They were the watchmen, each paid twenty pounds a year to patrol the streets at night, and they broke the nocturnal quiet with their sonorous reminders of time and weather. When they captured thieves, they consigned them to the Watch House. This stood on the site of the present Market, but it cannot have been a solid struc-ture, for once when they returned in the morning, three prisoners locked up the previous night, had escaped by the simple expedient of removing the roof.

The watchmen's appointment followed an Act of Parliament of 1766, relating to the government of the parish of Richmond, and trustees—the Minister, churchwardens, justices of the peace and other responsible residents, met at the "Sign of the Greyhound" in Great Street to discuss their new duties. Sir Charles Asgill was their chairman.

They levied two annual rates; one for the relief of the poor, the other, never to exceed one and sixpence in the pound, was for the maintenance of highways. The first local attempt at public street lighting in 1772, resulted in an order for one hundred oil-lamps at five shillings and threepence each. Solomon Brown, operating from Duke's Lane, was appointed street cleaner at a salary of seven pounds yearly. He was no ordinary dustman, for according to the Land Tax Books for the period, he paid heavy taxes.

A commission was set up to investigate the local workhouse, then situated in a building called Rump Hall in the Petersham Road. Rump Hall, which had a "banqueting-house", was mentioned in the Court Rolls in 1649. It had seventy-two inmates, paid some pensions and its budget of £752 a year included the purchase of 124 barrels of beer. Beef was supplied to the workhouse at two shillings, and mutton at two and eightpence the stone. A second Act of Parliament, relating to Richmond, was passed in 1785, when the government was entrusted to the Vestry. As a result of this Act, King George was empowered to close up the ancient highway, Love Lane, which divided the Richmond and Kew Gardens, although this does not appear to have been effected for some years. In return he repaired the road from Kew that ran to the "Bear" (the "Brown Bear") in Richmond at his own expense. He also gave the land on the Hill, rising from Pesthouse Common—a small pest-house or isolation hospital had been set up there in Stuart times—for a new workhouse and paid for its building. Queen Charlotte sent feather-beds for the comfort of the sick, old inmates.

The most distinguished of these was John Dodd, the "Father of English Violin Bow Makers", who was the first craftsman in England to adopt Toute's improvements. He would not take a pupil, for he did not want the secret of his pattern known. He lived at Kew, and although he was always hard at work, he remained a poor man, glad of occasional financial assistance from his patrons. Grove condemns as a legend the statement that he refused £1000 in return for the secret of his craft. He was eighty-seven years old in 1839 when he died in the Richmond Workhouse.

This Georgian edifice was rebuilt at the end of the nineteenth century, and in recent years has been transformed into a hospital. To the left of the entrance gate, under a picturesque cupola and a clock set in a stone pediment, a tablet inscribed with old-fashioned lettering, commemorates the Royal benefactor.

The mid-eighteenth century was a period of much local change.

Mr. Halford moved the "Castle" from its Jacobean premises in the
town to an old mansion in Hill Street. In 1766 the Theatre Royal
appeared on the Green (on the site of the present Garrick House).
Commissioned by a Mrs. Horn for the actor James Dance, son of
the City of London architect, it was built by Saunderson, the master
carpenter of Drury Lane, and was regarded as a model of elegance:
boxes formed a crescent, and light wall panelling replaced the
customary gingerbread stucco. On the opening night Garrick's
prologue declared:

> The ship now launched, with necessaries stored
> Rigged, manned, well-built, and a rich freight on board,
> All ready, tight and trim, from head to poop,
> And by commission made a royal sloop,
> May Heaven from tempests, rocks and privateers,
> Preserve the Richmond! Give her, boys, three cheers. . . .

"The ship", indeed, was set brilliantly upon its course, and during
the next few decades the leading actors in an interesting period of
British drama, appeared on its boards—Macready the Elder, Charles
Matthews, Mrs. Jordan, Vestris and Edmund Kean. Even the
great Sarah Siddons, in response to the residents' special request,
gave a performance, playing the part of Lady Randolph in the
tragedy *Douglas*.

But the old Playhouse on the Hill was doomed, despite efforts
to keep it open, and by 1774 the building had become the meeting-
house of Protestant Dissenters. When the Playhouse opened for its
new season in 1766, the manager, Mr. Shuter, recited these lines:

> Welcome, ye generous, polite and fair
> Who to our lowly roof this night repair;
> Who come, invited by our humble bill,
> To the old theatre on Richmond Hill:
> Where to those guests whose taste not over nice is,
> We serve up common fare—at common prices.
> No cornice here, no frieze to feast your eyes on,
> No galleries on Doric pillars rise,
> No gaudy paintings on the roof we dwell in,
> To break your necks with looking towards the ceiling;

No theatre we boast superbly built,
A gingerbread round O, a cockpit gilt,
But a plain booth, of boards ill-put together.
To raise a stage and keep out wind and weather.

The expert propagandist may detect a subtle tendency in these words to advertise the splendid theatre on the Green. Their author was George Colman the Elder, dramatist and stage-manager. He lived in the Vineyard until, inheriting a fortune from Lord Bath, he built a house by the river, overlooking the ferry. In 1766, writing to Colman who was abroad, Garrick stated, "Saunderson tells me they have laid the timbers for the first floor of your house at Richmond. It rises magnificently to the ferry passengers; you will be surprised to find yourself master of a château at your return."

Colman called his new home Bath House; a subsequent owner, Samuel Paynter restyled it Camborne House, and later, occupied by a Dowager Duchess of Northumberland, it became North-umberland House. To this last name, as the premises of the Richmond Club, it adheres. Some of its original decorations have survived such as the moulded ceilings and it has one splendid mahogany door. In former days its front entrance overlooked the river and two posts at the end of its grounds indicate the beginning of its drive. In *Random Records*, Colman the Younger, described how his father, looking at the view from his windows, often used to murmur a pet phrase—"all its shepherds were in silk". He loved to watch the ferry, plying between the banks, but later he was heard lamenting, for this time-honoured form of transport was to be replaced by a bridge.

Yes, like Kew Ferry, this one vanished, leaving Twickenham Ferry, which crossed from that town to Ham House, to become the theme of a romantic ballad. The building of Richmond Bridge, for which the ferry lessee, Mr. Windham, obtained official sanction, was preceded by bitter local controversy. Far-sighted residents declared that the best place for it was Water Lane, where it would link up with the route to London, and, as was proved in after years, their objections were well-founded. The obelisk outside the "King's Head", once a small inn called "Ferry House", reminds us in its inscription that the bridge was begun in 1774 and opened in 1777. Paine and Couse were its architects and its five main arches ex- tended 300 feet. The *Gentleman's Magazine* described it as a simple, but elegant structure built of Portland stone and considered that it was an ornament to the landscape. It cost £26,000 most of which was raised on tontine shares of £100 each, repaid as an annuity. The toll-fares were two shillings and sixpence for a coach, berlin or chaise drawn by six horses, decreasing in scale according to the number of steeds; a foot passenger paid a halfpenny or a penny if he trundled a wheelbarrow.

Richmond Bridge(49) was widened in 1937, and although its attractive hump, interspersed by deep bays, was flattened slightly in the process, its pearl stonework retains the grace which has been admired by artists through the decades. To Turner it appeared to be ivory-tinted, as he painted it in water-colours one warm, autumnal day, when the trees flamed gold, copper and bronze, the Hill shimmered in its green setting and low, white clouds sailed beneath a turquoise sky.

4

The lad, William Cobbett, in a blue smock, his untidy stockings tied up with red garters, looked so comical as he swept leaves near the Pagoda, that the young Princes burst out laughing as they passed by—mirth Cobbett never forgot. King George, too, was amused by the odd-looking boy, and when he was told that he had tramped across Surrey from Farnham to work in the beautiful Royal Gardens, directed that his services were to be retained. But William, who had spent his supper-money, his last threepence, at the end of the long tramp on a second-hand copy of *Tale of a Tub*, was fetched home by his father.

His brief stay occurred soon after George III had moved to Kew House in 1772, and Richmond Lodge was demolished. The Royal children lodged in houses round Kew Green, which, as Mrs. Papendiek remembered, changed its aspect slightly in 1776, when property was sold by the Crown and a number of small houses were demolished. Her father, Mr. Albert, who had come with Queen Charlotte to England, was able to acquire his own home for £400. Previously he had rented the Little Red House (now Beaconsfield) from Francis Engleheart, who according to the Burrell Survey, owned it in 1771.

Francis Engleheart, first member of the gifted family to settle in Kew, was a modeller of plaster ceilings. He married Anne Dawes and they lived at No. 23, Kew Green, where their son, George, the miniature painter, was born. In 1773 Francis died; George settled in Denmark House, which then included its semi-detached neighbour, and his brother, Thomas, a wax modeller, lived close by. Mrs. Engleheart, presumably Francis's widow, was in the Little Red House in 1777. Towards the end of the century it was tenanted by Mrs. Clementina Jacobi Sobieski Schnell. She was the daughter of Colonel Allen Macdonald, one of the first to greet Bonnie Prince Charlie when he set foot on Scotland's mainland. Macdonald joined the exiled House of Stuart in France, married a French-woman and their daughter, Mrs. Schnell, asserted that she was the godchild of the Old Pretender and his wife, Clementine Sobieska.

Mrs. Schnell, whose portrait was executed by John Cox Dillman Engleheart, lived in the Little Red House for over fifty years, and then met with a fatal accident—she set her crinoline alight and died in the flames. She was buried in Kew churchyard and her tomb was designed to resemble the Stuart Memorial in St. Peter's, Rome, but the romantic inscription on it is now almost obliterated.

The red bricks of Beaconsfield glow warmly across Kew Green, and its present owner states that the date 1668 is seen on the roof, indicating the year the house was built. Mrs. Schnell's accident occurred in a stone room, where small Tudor roses appear between the consoles in the cornice and in the decorative borders on its Adam green walls. The beautifully modelled ceiling, centring a sunburst, dates from a later period.

Colonel Gwynn, a Royal equerry, lived near the Little Red House. His wife was Mary Horneck, the Jessamy Bride, adored by Oliver Goldsmith, painted by Reynolds, referred to by Fanny Burney, who commented on her beauty and charming manners. Ferry Lane was known as Myer's Lane, for Jeremiah Myer, who designed George III's profile for the new coinage of 1761, occupied the corner house. His neighbour was Kirby, Clerk of the Works.

This ex-coach painter from Ipswich, who became an architect and an artist, had a famous daughter, Mrs. Sarah Trimmer. She was regarded as a model housewife, for she educated her twelve children personally and did not permit her duties as schoolmarm to interfere with her domestic work. When she was forty she began to write pious books, and some of them became best-sellers.

Gainsborough came to the neighbourhood to be near his friend Kirby, who, much to his grief, died soon after his arrival. He painted little Miss Haverfield in her quaint cape and cartwheel hat, and the portrait graces the Wallace Collection. She was the granddaughter of John Haverfield, Superintendent of the Royal Gardens, whose home Haverfield House, stands near the old, but rebuilt, "Coach and Horses". Incidentally, Gainsborough found other juvenile models in the neighbourhood—the boy, Jack Hill, and the little girl with the dog under her arm, whom he met on Richmond Hill.

In the mid-eighteenth century, the centre building of the present Herbarium was the home of Robert Hunter and the intricately carved oak balusters of the staircase which leads to the library, is a relic of his ownership. Lely's cottage, demolished in the first half of this century, stood in Hunter's grounds. Hunter House, occupied later by George III's unpopular son, the Duke of Cumberland and King of Hanover, was known subsequently as Hanover House.

The iron railing outside the Herbarium, cutting across the Green, indicates the site that George IV took from the parishioners to incorporate into the Royal Gardens—William IV returned it to the people. Near by, the yellow stock and red bricks and the green copper dome of St. Anne's rise pleasantly across the landscape. The church evolved gradually through the eighteenth and nineteenth centuries. An Act of Parliament of 1769 established the chapelries of Kew and Petersham as one vicarage, and in 1770, with J. J. Kirby as architect, the nave was lengthened, the north and south aisles added. But at that time the south aisle was separated for use as a school and the sextoness's lodging, and was not incorporated into the church until 1810. During this extension, the gallery, built by George III for his large family, was lengthened—the hatchments we see here recall these Hanoverian princes. The west end with the portico, was designed by Jeffrey Wyatville and paid for with a legacy left for that purpose by William IV.

Kew's records are incomplete for there was a curious robbery in the church in 1845, when an iron chest containing certain registers was stolen. The mystery of their disappearance has never been explained.

5

Mrs. Papendiek described entertainments at Kew—balls and firework displays organised to amuse the Royal children when lesson books were closed. During the summer months it was fashionable for water-parties to tie up their boats outside the Gardens and serenade the King and Queen. The painter Zoffany, who lived on the other side of Kew Bridge, at Strand-on-the-Green, sailed up with Johann Christian Bach, Madame Bach and Bach's pupil, the singer, Miss Cantilo and they gave lively concerts. The abolitionist, Granville Sharpe and his brothers anchored their yacht and also provided musical entertainment.

The happy life of the Royal Family, the halcyon days ended when the Prince of Wales (the future George IV) attained manhood and his brief romance with the actress, Perdita, Mrs. Robinson, opened in the moonlit Gardens. He, Florizel, wrapped in a long cloak, waited until Perdita was led to him through a private entrance in the wall. The lights of Hell House (it stood by Cambridge Cottage, but has since been destroyed) shone upon the Prince's revels until dawn. Florizel, inviting Perdita to dine with him at the "Star and Garter" on Richmond Hill, instructed her, if she arrived first, to order the dinner, telling her that he preferred the roast beef of Old England, for, in spite of his parentage, he was "an Englishman, every inch of him". Mrs. Papendiek, referring to the Prince's removal from Kew, stated: "The people of Richmond, on hearing of the preparations that were going on in Windsor, now came forward to offer the land that had been refused, even to entreaty; but it was too late."

Towards the end of 1788, the Kew people, who had a sincere affection for the King, always generous to needy parishioners, were distressed to hear that, mentally deranged, he was living in Kew

140

House, secluded from his family. The following February Fanny Burney had her memorable experience, when he saw her in the Gardens, chased her up alleys and round bushes, finally caught and kissed her, and entered into a long, characteristic monologue. A few weeks later the gloom had dispersed, he was better, and holding the little Princess Amelia's hand, stood at a window, admiring a decoration, a purple transparency with gilt tassels, set up to celebrate his recovery.

In September 1789, the King opened Kew's second bridge. Constructed of stone brought from the Purbeck quarries, it was placed a few yards lower down the river than its predecessor. The first bridge was still standing but its wooden arches were rotten and it could no longer be repaired. The new one took six years to build: James Paine's original designs had to be modified owing to excessive estimates, and his plans for placing four equestrian statues on arches over the toll-houses were scrapped. His ten-arched bridge, with its graceful balustrade, survived until the end of the nineteenth century, when it was replaced by the streamlined granite structure, opened in 1904 by King Edward VII.

It is said that George III's dislike of Kew House, dated from his detention there during his illness, and in 1802, once again he ordered the housebreakers to work and today only a sundial on a lawn marks the site where the house stood. Wyatt was commissioned to design a Gothic palace, to be built opposite unlovely Brentford. Turrets and towers appeared, introducing an unreal, medieval note, out of harmony with the current, progressive spirit. But only its shell was erected, for its progress was hampered by the King's frequent illnesses. It stood there until George IV, who thought it in execrable taste, had it destroyed.

The public shared this opinion: walking past it one day, the author-publisher, Sir Richard Phillips, compared it to the Bastille. On that occasion he saw something else of interest—a disabled ex-sailor had chalked representations of every one of the Royal Navy's 800 ships on the walls of Kew Gardens. The display covered a mile and a half, each ship was named and its guns numbered.

Their former home vanished, the Gothic palace unfinished, the Dutch House (34) became the residence of the Royal family at Kew.

From that time this gabled mansion, its Flemish bond bricks glowing warmly at the end of the Broad Walk, has had the inappropriate title of Kew Palace. Queen Victoria opened it to the public to commemorate the Diamond Jubilee, and then admission was free, but now we each pay one shilling to explore it. If we imagine we are going to wander through sumptuous rooms, we shall be disappointed, for here is none of the splendour of Hampton Court, the glitter of Ham House.

Over the stout doorway the initials "F.S.C." and the year 1631, indicate that it was built then by a merchant, Samuel Fortrey, whose wife's name was Catherine. He acquired the site from the Portman family, who had bought Lord Leicester's Dairie House. The Dutch House was built on the foundations of the first mansion—a beautiful Gothic crypt with a low, vaulted roof, and at one end, a perpendicular arch. This is not open to the public, but it is admirably preserved by the Ministry of Works.

Queen Caroline rented the Dutch House, which was bought later by the Royal family. It forms the background to Philip Mercier's picture of Frederick, Prince of Wales, playing the violoncello to his sisters. Frederick's crest and monogram appear on some of the heavy brass locks in the rooms: these may have been removed from Kew House when it was destroyed but the Prince lived in the Dutch House before his marriage and William Kent adapted it—the mullions were replaced by sash windows.

Today the rooms are labelled as they were used during the last phase of the Royal family's life at Kew. The King's Library on the ground floor has seventeenth-century panelling and ornamental woodwork of the period over the mantelpiece. A specimen from the future George IV's copybook, is preserved, with other souvenirs, in this room. The Prince's delineation of the words "Conscious Innocence", at a tender age, is shapely and indicates the future connoisseur of the arts. The Tudor linenfold panelling in the Library anteroom is believed to be a relic from the Dairie House.

The King's Dining-Room has a fine grate: some of the fireplaces in the Dutch House are of first-rate eighteenth-century craftsmanship, but others are negligible. A great open rose plastered in the ceiling of this room dates from Fortrey's occupation and so does the low ceiling in the Queen's Boudoir on the first floor. Here the motif is the Five Senses, illustrated by women in different attitudes—the centre medallion, for example, shows Hearing, represented by a woman with a guitar. The grey marble pillars with alabaster capitals, flanking the immense blocked-up chimney-piece in the Queen's Drawing-Room is Jacobean.

The rooms lead into one another, their wainscoting painted white, the walls above, apple green, and there are deep recessed window-seats. These apartments always wore a homely air and in 1816, Mary Lamb—she and Charles were shown round the house by an old woman who had been there twenty-six years—thought the furniture she saw exceedingly plain.

Today they are sparsely furnished with odd Georgian pieces and much of the upholstery is shabby and faded. Pictures comprise studies of birds, flowers and fruit and heavily varnished landscapes. George IV's favourite shaggy black and white dog stares with bulbous eyes from a canvas on the wall of the ground-floor passage. Upstairs there are many engravings of George III and his family, including a quota of elderly men with paunches, relieved by the wistful loveliness of the little Princess Amelia, and the charming Prince Octavius, who died in childhood.

Queen Charlotte worked the tapestry chairs, arranged near the harpsichord Shudi made in 1740 for Frederick, Prince of Wales. A volume of the Queen's poems, printed privately, is open revealing her as a mediocre verse-writer, although her sentiments were admirable. An example of her artistic talent, a sketch of a cottage, is exhibited on the ground floor. She did not intend this unfinished specimen to be inspected by generations of her descendants' subjects, and she threw it away, but an obsequious prelate retrieved and treasured it. Letters written by her children as adults, are kept in glass cases—spidery handwriting, faded ink and yellowing paper.

Here, we feel, is a great opportunity lost: with discrimination, rearrangement, articles added, their significance explained, the Dutch House could rank as a notable museum of Georgian pieces. Yet, despite its deficiencies as a showplace, the house fascinates. If ever the atmosphere of the last occupants lingered in their old home, it does here, in these rooms, impregnated with the secrets of the Guelph dynasty.

The Dutch House knew its last great day on July 11th, 1818, when in the Queen's Drawing-Room, the middle-aged Dukes of Clarence and Kent were married by the Archbishop of Canterbury to their German brides—Princess Adelaide of Saxe-Meiningen and Victoria, Princess of Leiningen, who became the mother of Queen Victoria. Queen Charlotte was too ill to attend the banquet in the King's Dining-Room or the alfresco tea-party by the Pagoda, presided over by the Prince Regent. A few months later she died in that house, as is recorded on the brass tablet placed in her bedroom by her granddaughter, Queen Victoria.

By that time many changes had come to Kew and familiar figures had vanished. Gainsborough, as he had wished, had been buried by Kirby's side in the churchyard on the Green, and Meyer had become Kirby's neighbour in death, as he had been in life.

In the last summer of the eighteenth century, the French writer, Chateaubriand, spending the season at Richmond, went to the Royal Gardens. He was amused by a fantastic animal which had just joined the Royal menagerie—he had never before seen a kangaroo.

6

In 1791, the *Universal British Directory* of trade, commerce and manufacture, devoted a few pages to an account of Richmond. It indicated vaguely where prominent residents lived—the Duke of Clarence, Richmond Hill, the Duke of Buccleuch, Under the Hill. Buccleuch had inherited the Montagu estate and the *Directory* noted that his grounds on the Hill were connected by a subterranean passage to his house. The Russian ambassador, Voronozov, found his name anglicised to simple "Count Warren". Reference was made to Lady Diana Beauclerk's cottage and the fact that she had decorated one of her rooms there with lilac and other flowers in the same way as she had treated her former residence at Twickenham.

Lady Diana, *née* Spencer, whose second husband was Topham Beauclerk, descendant of Charles II and Nell Gwynn, was the favourite granddaughter of Sarah, Duchess of Marlborough. She

45 The Centre Block built about 1727 by Lord Pembroke; the wings
designed later by Robert Morris

46 Shows the "Improvement" made to the Garden by Humphry Repton about 1816

Both from Repton "Fragments . . . of Landscape Gardening"

WHITE LODGE, RICHMOND PARK

47 Richmond: Cedar Grove, rebuilt in the early nineteenth century

48 Regency Houses by Cholmondeley Walk

lived in the little white house—Reynolds used to point it out to his
friends for he could see it from his windows—known as Devonshire
Cottage, from which Devonshire Lodge has evolved. (Georgiana,
Duchess of Devonshire, who occupied the cottage for a time, gave
it its name.)

Lady Di, as her friends called her, was a gifted prolific artist and
her children were models for her cupids and baby Pans, the setting,
the glades of Richmond Park. Many of her drawings were engraved
by Bartolozzi, and, sometimes foxed, but still extremely charming,
they are often seen in old-fashioned houses. She designed for
Wedgwood who used her decorations on his china and she painted
furniture. Horace Walpole wrote enthusiastically of the lilac festoons she had executed on the walls of her Twickenham home, but
he deplored that they had been carried out in water-colours on
paper and therefore, must perish. The same fate lay in store for the
Richmond ones.

The *Universal British Directory* considered the "Castle" and the
"Star and Garter" very elegant taverns. About this period the landlord of the "Castle" was Benjamin Topham, whose widow, inheriting the property, became Mrs. Thomas Forty. She was said to be the
heroine of Sheridan's famous toast, "Fair, Fat and Forty": Sheridan,
one of Lady Di's friends, resided for some years at Downe House
on the Terrace, and his children Jane Georgiana and Thomas
Berkeley were christened in Petersham Church. Downe House
is today characterised by blue blinds, claret paint and deep yellow
stock bricks and it is possible that when Sheridan lived there, it
comprised also the houses on either side of it.

The *Directory* informed readers that the mail arrived daily at
Richmond at nine o'clock: the tiny post-office was kept by Robert
Rowland in his grocery shop in King Street, and after his death,
his daughter, Nancy, became proud postmistress. Coaches set out
frequently for London, and during the summer they ran ten times
daily from the "Old Ship".

The town was served well by professions and trades. Mrs. Budd
kept a Ladies' Boarding-School in the vicinity of the Green:
Benjamin and Thomas Budd were professional musicians—
Thomas became associated with the Theatre Royal. In 1791, Mr.

Lewis Briggs gave young ladies dancing lessons, and Mr. William Tibbs taught them music. Matrons patronised Francis Darnell's tea warehouse in King Street, children chose toys from James Moore's shop and C. Penfold had the distinction of being silk stocking cleaner to the Duke of Clarence. William Johnson made stays for local Beaux Brummels and William Viney specialised in muffins, those delicacies introduced from France earlier in the century. An incredible number of hairdressers and perfumers rivalled one another in this Arcadia-on-Thames.

But the best impression of late eighteenth-century Richmond is gained from Horace Walpole's letters. How he loved the place—his metropolis, where he met all the best people! Sometimes he seems wistful that his Gothic "castle" is not perched on the summit of the Hill. He mentions local floods, the highwaymen and an air balloon he sees over the Hill, but. . . . "Mrs. Hobart was going by and her coiffure prevented my seeing it alight." The Hon. Mrs. Hobart, whom he nicknamed "Mother Hubbard", was often the butt for his humour. She lived in Sans Souci, Ham Common, where, "having made as many conquests as the King of Prussia", she had borrowed the name of that hero's villa for her house. Walpole went to a rural breakfast she held in her grounds, transformed for the occasion into a French village. Madame du Barry was a guest and he found her "*un peu passée*".

At Petersham he visited Lady Julia Penn, whom he called "the late Queen of Pennsylvania", for she was the widow of Thomas Penn of the American colony. Members of this family, the great-grandchildren of William Penn, lived at Richmond until the mid-nineteenth century and were buried in Petersham churchyard. Mary Penn married Samuel Paynter of Camborne House.

While they were abroad, Walpole wrote frequently to his young friends, the Misses Mary and Agnes Berry, whom he called playfully his "beloved spouses". "I am not wont to listen to the batteries on each side of me at Hampton Court and Richmond; but in your absence, I shall turn a less deaf ear to them in hopes of gleaning something that may amuse you." What an understatement of fact! From the time he settled at Twickenham he gossiped about his friends on the other side of the river. As early as 1749, he complained to Sir Horace Mann about the habits of certain noblemen he knew who spent their week-ends playing cards at Richmond. He saw them one Sunday, lounging at the door of No. 17, the Green, famed throughout the eighteenth century as the Italian, then the London Coffee House, with stables and outhouses in Duke Street.

Walpole's dear niece, Charlotte, married the fifth Earl of Dysart, an eccentric, churlish peer, who, disliking visitors, barricaded his house. Horace crossed the river, probably by the famous Twicken-ham ferry, to see the new Countess, whose portrait by Reynolds, hanging in the Great Hall of Ham House, shows a handsome young woman in a white satin gown, a white satin slipper emerging from its hem. Ham House, its view of the Thames purposely cut off by the heavy trees which grew around it, depressed Walpole. He thought the ancient furniture dreary and decayed, and, "Every minute I expected to see ghosts sweeping by; ghosts I would not give sixpence to see, Lauderdales, Talmachs and Maitlands . . . you are locked out and locked in, and after journeying all round the house as you do round an old French fortified town, you are at last admitted through the stable-yard to creep along a dark passage by the house-keeper's room, and so by a back-door into the great hall. He (Lord Dysart) seems as much afraid of water as a cat, for though you might enjoy the Thames from every window of three sides of the house, you may tumble into it before you would guess it is there."

He visited another eccentric peer, the Duke of Queensberry, the notorious "Old Q", who, after Lady Cowper's death, bought Cholmondeley House, known henceforth as Queensberry House. Walpole disparaged his host's pictures, sighed for a glimpse of the Palace of long ago, but met interesting people there. One of his fellow-guests was Mrs. Emma Hart, later Lady Hamilton: ". . . she sang . . . her attitudes were a whole theatre of graces and various expressions". At Queensberry House he often saw his friend, George Selwyn, who shared with the Duke the unusual guardian-ship of the little Maria Fagniani, her paternity uncertain.

"Old Q" left Richmond, angered by the townspeople's refusal to allow him to enclose Cholmondeley Walk in his grounds. His house, inherited by Miss Fagniani who married the Marquis of Hertford, was demolished about 1830 when its marble entrance

149

hall and staircase, which wound up to the white and gold ballroom, were removed. A second Queensberry House was built in the grounds, sited at a greater distance from the river, and designed like an Italian villa. This, too, was destroyed, to make room for the flats built this century, but it achieved fame for Baroness Orczy admitted that she had described it as the Richmond home of *The Scarlet Pimpernel*.

Walpole's letters contained many allusions to the Duke of Clarence (the future William IV), who was popular in the neighbourhood: ". . . he pays his bills regularly, locks up his doors at night that his servants may not stay out late and never drinks but a few glasses of wine". Clarence occupied four houses in the locality at different times: he bought the Petersham Lodge Harrington had owned; he had a mansion in the lower end of the town, and he resided at Clarence House in the Vineyard. He rented Ivy Hall, which with its amusing contrasts in window styles, resembles a small fortress from its site, overlooking the river, above the Bridge. "The Duke of Clarence has a house in the middle of Richmond with nothing but a short green apron to the river."

The Duke's first companion was a Miss Polly Finch, who, it was gossiped, left him because he bored her by reading aloud. Then he was joined by the popular actress, Mrs. Jordan ("Nell of Clarence", Walpole nicknamed her), whose performance at the Theatre Royal, especially in *The Country Girl*, delighted local audiences. "A favourite comic actress, if old Goody Rumour is to be trusted," commented a contemporary journal, "has thought it proper to place herself under the protection of a distinguished Sailor who dropped anchor before her last summer at Richmond."

Walpole chortled, the less sophisticated were scandalised, when it was announced, outside the Theatre Royal, that Mrs. Jordan would not be appearing that night, because it was the Duke's birthday: she had to do the honours to the Prince of Orange who was dining with him.

The Duke's birthday on August 23rd was celebrated each year by a local regatta, and in 1791, Walpole, with Clarence, Lady Diana Beauclerk, and her brother, Lord Robert Spencer, watched the events from the great room in the "Castle". "The scene both up and down the river was what only Richmond upon earth can exhibit", he wrote, describing the crowds in the green velvet meadows, the gay craft on the Thames, the ball held that night at the "Castle", and the town illuminated with the Duke's cypher. He did not go to the ball, but returned to Richmond to call on the "French ladies on the Green". They were Madame de Boufflers and her daughter, the Comtesse Amélie, "who sometimes carries her harp, on which they say she plays better than Orpheus". With many of their compatriots these distinguished refugees, sheltered in the Thames Valley from French Revolutionary storms. Calling on them one Sunday, Walpole found they were out: they had gone to the house of their neighbour, Lord Fitzwilliam, to hear his organ.

The seventh Viscount Fitzwilliam of Merrion lived in the mansion, set in spacious grounds, on the west side of the Green, bought by his grandfather, Sir Matthew Decker, after Sir Charles Hedges had vacated it. Decker, a wealthy Dutch merchant, had enlarged and added a splendid salon, where in 1720, he entertained George I. On this occasion, he set before the monarch a pineapple grown on his Richmond estate. It is sometimes stated that it was the first English cultivated pineapple, a fact disproved by Dankerts' painting of Rose, the Royal gardener, presenting Charles II with the premier home-grown fruit of the species. (There is a fine replica of this painting in Ham House.) Nevertheless, Sir Matthew was so proud of his pineapples that he had one, a large, handsome specimen, painted by T. Netscher, and the picture is now in the Fitzwilliam Museum, Cambridge. Decker is credited as the man who intro-duced goldfish into England, and he had a remarkable courtyard to his house, made of Dutch clinker bricks, designed like a star.

He also bought valuable paintings, some of which were hung in the new salon. Among them was Vinkeboons' picture of early Stuart Richmond (to which I have referred previously), stated originally to have hung in the Palace.

There are some interesting portraits of this family in "The Founder's Corner" of the Fitzwilliam Museum. Here, on the side, is a delightful study by Jan de Meyer of Decker's four little daughters. The portraits of Catherine Decker as Lady Fitzwilliam—she wears pearl-trimmed white satin and her hair is powdered lightly—and of her husband are separated by that of their son, Richard, the founder of the famous museum. It was painted by Joseph Wright of Derby, when the future seventh viscount was a nineteen-year-old under-graduate at Cambridge, and he wears a rich gown over a blue suit. Below is the only other existing portrait of him, an unsatisfactory painting by Henry Howard, showing him as a benevolent-looking elderly man, a bound manuscript on his knee.

This was executed, presumably, at Richmond where the bachelor Lord Fitzwilliam collected treasures. To the pictures he inherited from his grandfather, he added others, including the famous Titian, formerly called "Philip II and the Princess d'Eboli," and now labelled "Venus and Cupid with a Man playing a Lute", which he purchased from the Orleans collection for £1,000. His medieval manuscripts included many Books of Hours, his remarkable prints a fine collection of Rembrandt etchings. His 10,000 books were judged, at the time of his death, to be worth £24,000. Deeply interested in music, he acquired some Handel manuscripts and the celebrated *Virginal Book*, which includes the best existing contemporary collection of seventeenth-century keyboard music.

Fitzwilliam, who came to be regarded as another local eccentric peer, seldom left his home and was a recluse, but he permitted the interested to visit his famous library. He bequeathed his magnificent possessions to the University of Cambridge with £100,000 to build a museum. His death occurred at the age of seventy in February 1816 and in the following April the *Gentleman's Magazine* reported the arrival of wagons laden with his bequests at Cambridge. His former valet, William Key, became the first custodian of the treasures, displayed in temporary premises until the opening of the museum in 1848.

The Founder was buried in the Decker vault outside the Richmond Parish Church, above which is the pyramided sarcophagus identified by the late Mrs. K. A. Esdaile as the work of Peter Schee-maker or Scheemakers. The house on the Green, known subse-quently as Pembroke House, was inherited by his relatives, the Pembrokes of Wilton. It was demolished in the mid-nineteenth century and replaced by the present Pembroke Villas, its ground used to build the railway line to Twickenham.

The only other house on the west side of the Green in Fitzwilliam's day—the one occupied by Madame de Boufflers—was Cedar Grove, which stands in a beautiful garden with a Queen Anne summer-house. This house was rebuilt in late Georgian style in 1813 and, situated approximately on the site of "Ye King's Bakehouse", has interesting, ancient cellars. In one there are indications that at some time in bygone centuries, it was used as a secret chapel. During this early nineteenth-century reconstruction, workmen cutting into the cellars found two antique silver spoons and some wine, estimated to be nearly 300 years old.

Other French *émigrés* in Richmond included the politician, de Lally-Tollendal who occupied a house with Madame d'Hénin, aunt of the Marquise de la Tour du Pin. At the instigation of this relative, the Marquise arrived in the town with her young family. Later she described her life there from 1798 to 1799, in the *Journal d'une Femme de Cinquante Ans*. She rented a small house, a "real jewel"—its staircase tucked away from the passage. This has been identified as No. 3, the Green, before its Gothic front was added. The rooms she occupied were under the aged gables. In the old part of this house, of late Elizabethan or early Jacobean origin, there is a narrow door in a ground-floor room. It conceals an unusual shaft that runs up to an attic and is built at the side of a wide, open, brick-backed fireplace: a first-floor room through which it passes shows another unusual fireplace—a four-centred Tudor arch, its spandrels embossed with vine leaves.

The names on tombstones in Richmond's Old Burial Ground in the Vineyard Passage, testify that many of the French refugees never returned to their native land. In 1793 they were permitted to open a chapel in the Vineyard, and this, it is believed, stood on the site of the courtyard of the present Roman Catholic church, dedi-cated to St. Elizabeth of Portugal. In 1824, its building was begun and it was handsomely endowed by Miss Doughty of Doughty House. (She also founded the Priory at Kew, which, however, was closed after her death.)

St. Elizabeth's, as it is seen today, is a combination of late Georgian and Renaissance styles, its façade surmounted by a green copper dome. Recently the interior has been redecorated in shades of Wedgwood blue and soft green, embellished with gold leaf. A modern mural, a dado executed in tempera—white figures on a deep blue ground—depicts the Stations of the Cross. The beautiful silver lamp came from the Royal Chapel at Lisbon and was the gift of the late ex-Queen Amelia of Portugal, who worshipped here during the many years she lived at Abercorn (since demolished) in the King's Road, Richmond.

Land on the Hill was growing valuable when St. Elizabeth's was built and six years later the Congregational Church was erected close to it. Richmond's oldest Noncomformist place of worship, the Bethlehem Independent Chapel, appeared in 1797 at the top of Church Terrace, and framed by tall bushes, preserves its original diminutive aspect. It was paid for by John Chapman, an ardent follower of the coal-heaver preacher, William Huntington, S.S.—the initials stood for "Sinner Saved"—who delivered the first sermon heard in the historic little building.

Chapter IX

NINETEENTH-CENTURY BACKGROUND

Nelson—Cardinal Newman's Childhood—Richmond Volunteers—Regency Houses—Lady Hamilton and the Marquis of Wellesley—Cardigan House Fête—Royal Watermen—Edmund Kean—The Misses Berry—The Railway—New Roads and Churches—Impressions of Distinguished Visitors—Dickens, Thackeray and George Eliot—Development of "Star and Garter"

I

ON the wet Sunday of September 10th, 1805, a few days before he sailed from Portsmouth, Admiral Nelson turned his chaise into Richmond Park, on his way to White Lodge to visit Lord Sidmouth. Dinner over, he traced on a small, round table the plan of action he intended to follow if he encountered the enemy fleet. A few weeks later Nelson was dead, and little John Henry Newman gazed from his bed in his home at Grey Court, Ham Street, off Ham Common, at the candles placed in the windows to celebrate the victory at Trafalgar.

In after life, Cardinal Newman's thoughts reverted to his child-hood's home, which he left at the age of seven to go to school. "I dreamed about it when a schoolboy as if it were paradise. It would be here where the angel faces appeared 'loved long since but lost awhile'", he wrote in a letter dated 1886. He described Grey Court, as "an old-fashioned place, the house may be the date of George II, a square hall in the middle and in the centre of it a pillar and rooms all around". John Henry, born when England was at war with France, must have seen coachmen, gardeners and footmen drilling on Ham Common—the Richmond Volunteers.

The first Richmond Volunteer Corps was formed in 1794, and in 1803, to increase local defence in case of a possible invasion, a meeting, with Lord Onslow as Lord-Lieutenant of Surrey in the chair, was held at the "Castle". Recruitments followed and the committee responsible for the Volunteers' funds, issued a quaintly worded appeal, reminding "opulent" residents that £400 were required for equipment. These predecessors of the Home Guard turned out for review on the Green in 1810, a smart body of men.

Lord Onslow, who once entertained the Prince Regent to breakfast—on that occasion there was a review of a regiment of Surrey Fencible Cavalry—lived at Onslow House (now Nos. 8, and 9, the Green). He is commemorated by Onslow Hall by the Little Green, the Romanesque-styled building, dating from 1857, and used as a cavalry college in mid-Victorian days. It has been restored recently for the Association of Engineering and Shipbuilding Draughtsmen, and cream paint and Suffolk white bricks have revived its dignity. Its new railings were executed by Kingston craftsmen.

Onslow died in 1814, the year the Richmond townspeople celebrated Napoleon's downfall: how they cheered as guns boomed across the river and the watermen, decked with white cockades and fleurs-de-lis, led a procession through the streets. First came "Louis XVIII" in robes, then a mock, chained "Boney", and finally "Joseph, ex-King of Spain" for whom a tattered Spanish coat had been provided. The "Star and Garter" was resplendent with uniforms, glittered with decorations as the Prince Regent, the Emperor Alexander I of Russia and the King of Prussia assembled for a banquet.

St. Helena Terrace, built over boathouses at the end of Friars Lane, recalls the incarceration of the French ogre in his Atlantic island. The bow-shaped windows of St. Helena House, its recessed doorway flanked by fluted Doric columns introduces a Cheltenham atmosphere into the river scene. Other contemporary houses are seen near by, behind Cholmondeley Walk. The first is Cholmondeley Cottage, a semi-octagonal house, its balcony supported by slender pillars. Two small glass cupolas illuminate the hall of Cholmondeley House, the third in this row, and the stairway, its slim wrought-iron balustrades decorated with tiny heads, leads to a bow-shaped room. Each of its three windows has a long, narrow balcony with a superb view of the Thames.

Waterloo Place also commemorated the great victory, for cottages appeared on the site of the unlovely spot, leading from World's End (The Quadrant), which had been known for centuries as the Black Ditch. One of its tiny, neat front gardens is dignified by the Royal

Arms, painted on the trade sign of a time-honoured family of local sweeps.

Nelson's legacy to his country, Lady Hamilton and the little girl Horatia, often stayed in Richmond after the Admiral's death. The first time they came they occupied the centre house in Heron Court, called Herring Court in their day. Emma's former home has the air of an old-fashioned doll's house, its short, steep roof perched over rose-red bricks, ornamented with heavy cream dressings. Its Queen Anne neighbour, Hotham House (later named after a groom-in-waiting at Kew Palace, and in the nineteenth century the country residence of Baron Heath, a Governor of the Bank of England), has a remarkable sixteenth-century Italian marble medallion inset in the wall of a ground-floor room. Its sculptor is unknown, and it is carved with a representation of the old hill city of Fiesole and the busts of Silla, Charlemagne and Totlas.

A single diminutive painted circle—from the ground it looks the size of a penny—is the sole survivor of former decoration in the octagonal ceiling of the entrance. This leads to a black and white marble paved hall, its dignity diminished by the words "Mind the Step" painted in bold letters. For Hotham House is occupied by local authority officials and during the Second World War thousands of residents tramped up that stately staircase, so reminiscent of pannered skirts.

Lady Hamilton was recognised at many of the leading social functions where another guest appeared who was also associated with a hero of the French war—the Duke of Wellington's brother, the Marquis of Wellesley. He owned the mansion on the Hill which later became the property of the Marquis of Lansdowne. Wellesley lent his grounds to the Dowager Countess of Cardigan when she held a fête in 1817 to celebrate the Prince Regent's birthday and a walk was cut through the two estates.

Lansdowne House has gone, but Cardigan House remains as the club premises of the disabled men who work in the British Legion Poppy Factory, making millions of artificial poppies each year for Remembrance Day. The estate, the site of the former Wells, has become a Poppy village, for homes for the men and their families have been built round the factory at the end of the grounds.

The club premises are usually pointed out as the home of the Earl of Cardigan who led the Charge of the Light Brigade at Balaclava, and Cardigan Road, on the opposite side of Richmond Hill, was named after the hero. At No. 8, the Rev. James Chesterton Bradley spent his last years. He was the last surviving link with the Brontë sisters, for in his youth he had been a curate near Haworth, and he was the original of Mr. Sweeting, characterised by Charlotte in *Shirley*. He died shortly before the First World War.

The façade of Cardigan House retains traces of its former elegance. It is centred by a recessed Venetian window, and above it appears another window, an oval garlanded by flowers. This is surmounted by an oblong plaque stuccoed with richly filled cornucopias.

This decoration is of special interest when we read in an account of the Royal fête, given by *Bell's Weekly Messenger*, that a horn of plenty, containing the most delicious grapes and peaches was placed before the Prince Regent when he arrived with his mother, Queen Charlotte. This entertainment took six weeks to prepare; the hostess had hoped to give the banquet in her grounds, but owing to uncertain weather, the tables were set in her salon. They were arranged by the Queen's confectioner, who prepared special biscuits for the occasion. The Royal guests strolled to the riverside and the Lord Mayor of London in the City Barge, stationed on the river, exchanged ceremonious bows across the Thames with the First Gentleman of Europe. Princess Charlotte drove with Prince Leopold from Claremont in an open carriage and received a tremen-dous ovation from street spectators, but she did not stay for the banquet. This was her last public appearance for the following November she died in childbirth.

The Cardigan House fête was the forerunner of other brilliant riverside entertainments. In 1833 the Duke of Buccleuch was host to William IV and Queen Adelaide when, according to a con-temporary newspaper report, ottomans were arranged on the riverside lawn which had been covered with a carpet. The Austrian diplomat, Prince Schwarzenberg, entertained 1,000 guests, who included the Royal Dukes and the Duke of Wellington, at the "Castle" in 1838 to celebrate Victoria's coronation. Elegant tem-porary pavilions were erected on the lawn of the hotel. This occasion was eclipsed in 1842 by the splendid fête the Duke of Buccleuch arranged for Queen Victoria and Prince Albert. The town of Richmond wore gala dress, decorated boats came up the river and the Twickenham bank was crowded with spectators who watched the finest firework display known in local history.

Novel forms of river craft were seen at Richmond in the early nineteenth century. In 1824, Mr. Julius of Old Palace Yard built the first canoe known in England and tested it on the Thames. From 1816 paddle steamers, their tall funnels belching clouds of black smoke, churned the water as they brought tourists from London. In the *Every Day Book*, William Hone described how they were patronised by international travellers: "The lively French, the philosophic German, the elegant Italian, the lofty Spaniard and the Cossack of the Don pronounce the prospect from the Hill, the most enchanting in Europe."

Sometimes, at low tide, the steamers were stranded for hours on the banks and these distinguished foreigners were rescued from temporary imprisonment by the local watermen. The Richmond watermen are folk with traditions and many are descended from families who have known this reach of the Thames for generations. The first reference, for example, to the Chitty family occurs in the Parish Registers in 1679. James Chitty became one of George IV's Royal Watermen and from that time, from generation to generation, his descendants have held similar appointments. Today Albert is Waterman to Queen Elizabeth II, and, like his forbears, he is a resplendent figure on official occasions. His uniform consists of a scarlet coat, gold-plated coats of arms at the back and at the front, scarlet breeches with gold buttons, scarlet stockings, black shoes, white gloves and a black velvet cap. The Royal Watermen are seen at a Coronation, at the Opening of Parliament, and, of course, when the Sovereign is rowed on the Thames in a State Barge.

James was a water-carrier and carried goods up and down from London, until more modern methods of transport resulted in dimin-ished trade and then he became parish beadle, constable, and assistant toll-keeper of the Bridge. Like the famous Elizabethan waterman-poet, Taylor, James was a verse-writer and the Chitty family treasure a printed sheet of his odes inspired by great national occasions.

159

His son Bob, who lived to be an old man and was a well-known riverside figure in the early years of this century, told many stories of his youth. The Duke of Buccleuch had a private laundry in the Petersham Road, and when the ducal family resided in London, the washing had to be taken down the Thames. Bob helped row the randan, heavy with laundry-boxes, which had to be hauled along Whitehall and up the stairs of Montagu House. He began to let boats out on hire: in those days they were green, unvarnished, two-headed and were called "the funnies". Young men did not deign to row, but, prim in top-hats and kid gloves, engaged Bob to take them to Eeel Pie Island for a spree in the dancing-salon. The old man used to say that in his young days women were considered fast if they as much as touched an oar.

Bob's descendants sigh for a return of the days when he told these tales—the gilded years before the First World War when men in immaculate flannels tendered golden sovereigns in payment. They long for a revival of river trade and they believe it would come if the young Queen, like Elizabeth I, travelled up the river in her State Barge, rowed by her resplendent Watermen.

In former days the watermen's haunt was the district round Water Lane, which echoed continually with the cry "Man to Horse", indicating that bargemen were required to haul barges to the next stage of their journey. They worked in teams, the leather straps round their shoulders attached to the towing-line, much, indeed, as Wyngaerde depicted them in the sixteenth century. Many of the river people lived in cottages near the "White Cross" Inn, built on the site of the Chapel of the Convent of Observant Friars. The "White Cross" has a rare, attractive fireplace in its bar: the conventional chimney is replaced by a window with a charming view.

The watermen were the soul of local activities in the early nineteenth century and Shrove Tuesday was Richmond's black day, for then they played a traditional football match in the main streets. Their opponents came from Michel's Row—it used to be called Night and Morning Row because one of its first cottages was built, unaided, by a Kew gardener who worked on it early in the morning and late into the night. Up and down went the football on Shrove Tuesday and the play grew rougher each hour. Shops were shut, windows barricaded and timid residents stayed indoors. The damage was always extensive but the watermen were angry when the Metropolitan Police, their jurisdiction extending to Richmond in 1840, banned the game.

The river people lost a good friend in 1833 when Edmund Kean died, for every year he gave them a wherry. Mrs. Chitty, a pew opener at the Parish Church at Kean's funeral, was horrified at the behaviour of the mob. Members of the theatrical profession stormed into the building as soon as the doors were opened: men and boys climbed to the roof and peeped through the little windows under the eaves. Arriving as the cortège passed into the church, Grimaldi the clown raised his hat and shouted, "Bravo, Teddy, you've drawn a full house to the last!"

Edmund Kean was a sick man when, two years before his death, he became actor⁄manager at the Theatre Royal. At first he attracted full houses, but his patrons diminished and box⁄office returns grew depressingly low. Robert Browning, passionate admirer of good acting, sometimes walked from London to see Kean's performances: young Shelley attended a play at Richmond and was disappointed. The future explorer, Richard Burton, taken to see *Richard III*, thought the audience seemed afraid of Kean.

Burton and his brother attended the Rev. Charles Delafosse's well⁄known school on the Little Green, but their memories were unfavourable: to Richard it seemed a kind of "Dotheboys Hall" and the portly Rev. Charles no more fit to be a schoolmaster than the "Great Cham of Tartary".

Sometimes they saw Kean, his small, bent figure wrapped in furs, walking slowly across the Green. Helen Faucit, a child at the time, was introduced to him and hearing she was fond of poetry, he asked her to go and recite to him—an invitation that remained unfulfilled by his death. Kean inspired Helen, who developed into a Shake⁄spearian actress, and she thought of him on the night before her first performance as Juliet, when she used his cottage by the Theatre Royal as a dressing⁄room. The young Helen spent a summer at Gothic House, the Green, and one of the Kembles went there frequently to coach her.

Kean's last months in his little cottage were tragic, as he drank brandy and brooded over his misfortunes. One night, his medical adviser, Dr. Smith, creeping into a room where the actor, accompanying himself, had been singing softly, noticed that the piano-keys were wet with tears.

Dr. Smith of Belle Vue, the Petersham Road, did not charge Kean for attendance, but some of his accounts, submitted to wealthy patients exist—written on long foolscap sheets, every preparation used is itemised. The leeches, the castor oil, the Epsom salts, the camphor julep he prescribed for the households of the Marquis of Wellesley and of Dorothea, Princess Lieven, ran into hundreds of pounds. The Princess, whose correspondence from Richmond is dated from about 1813 to 1833, thought it the most beautiful spot in England.

Madame de Staël was another distinguished foreigner who lived in the neighbourhood in the early nineteenth century. She rented the Gothic House in the Petersham Road, and she had been married secretly to her second husband, Count Albert de Rocca, before she arrived. She frequently entertained Talleyrand there, and another visitor was Tom Moore, who stayed at Lansdowne House. The Gothic House, like its neighbour Midhurst, was demolished in 1938 for road widening: Midhurst was celebrated as the home of the poetess Catherine Fanshawe, whose anagram on the letter "H" was considered so clever that for a time it was attributed to Byron. Sir Walter Scott admired Catherine's intellect, but her virtues, enumerated by her friends, indicate that the poetess of the Petersham Road was a prig. She reigned as queen over a literary circle, said to be so exclusive that not even the famous Misses Berry could penetrate it.

Mary and Agnes often deserted their Mayfair house and rented Devonshire Cottage from the Honourable Caroline Lamb. Janet Ross, Lady Duff-Gordon's granddaughter, was taken to tea there when she was very young and they were very old. Mary, the "Elderberry", who had prepared Walpole's works for publication, intimidated the child, but Miss Agnes was kind and plied her with cake. The little girl thought it quaint when the Misses Berry spoke primly of "a dish of tea". The celebrated sisters both died in 1852, when they were in their late eighties. They were buried in Petersham churchyard "amidst scenes which in life they had frequented and loved".

49   Richmond Bridge, 1774-77

James Paine and Kenton Couse, Architects

50   Richmond College, 1843

A. Trimen, Architect

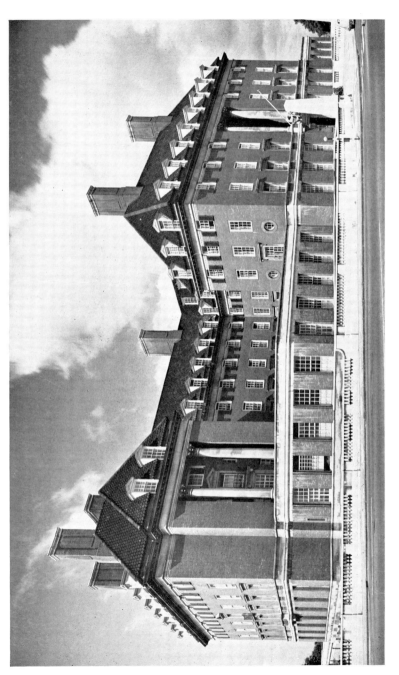

51 The Star and Garter Home (1924) on Richmond Hill

Sir Edwin Cooper, R.A., Architect

The first indication that Richmond would develop into a great dormitory town for London's workers, came in 1846, with the construction of the railway. The mere suggestion that this novel form of transport should be introduced was resisted firmly by the residents. "For whose particular accommodation is this expense and outlay to be made?" they asked in a petition sent to official quarters. "Will it offer a grand inducement for families of distinction to become residents? Is it thought that the village will be improved by the influx of visitors?"

The appeal was in vain. A "Gothic style" station was built at the end of the Little Green. On July 28th, 1846, a party of favoured travellers, seated in a train of sixteen carriages, drawn by the "Crescent" locomotive, left Vauxhall at five minutes past two. As it puffed into the Richmond terminus thirty-two minutes later, bells pealed, a brass band blared the National Anthem, and the pioneers passed beneath evergreen arches as they drove to the "Castle" Hotel for a banquet. The Lord Mayor of London, who, on this day of days, had arrived somewhat inappropriately by water in the City Barge, the "Maria Wood", called the toast: "Prosperity to the Richmond Railway."

Two years later the railway bridge spanned the Thames near Asgill House and linked Richmond with Staines and Windsor. Presently children, playing below on the towing-path, clapped their hands as a miniature train rumbled across the bridge, and nursemaids cried, "There goes the Queen's clean washing!" The Prince Consort had designed a model laundry, built by Cubitt, in the Kew Foot Road, and every day for the remainder of the Victorian era, the toy train transported the Queen's laundry to Windsor, Buckingham Palace or Osborne—everywhere Her Majesty resided, Balmoral excepted. An American author who penetrated the steamy, soapy atmosphere in the laundry's early days, eulogised the Royal mangle, which he thought the most perfect machine ever made. It cost sixty pounds.

In early Victorian days, honeysuckle and dog-roses still grew in the lanes up Richmond Hill. Black Horse Lane, commonly spoken of as "Muddy Lane", had only four houses along it until 1845, and then Mr. E. S. Cole laid out the site and commodious villas appeared on either side of the handsome, new thoroughfare—the Queen's Road. Many of the streets between this road and the town were only developed in the eighteen-seventies by the London publisher, Mr. John Maxwell. He named some of them after the characters featured in the popular books written by his novelist wife, Miss Braddon—Audley Road, Marchmont Road.

Between the years 1841 to 1843, the Wesleyan College, a Bath stone Perpendicular style building, arose at the top of the Hill. This is now Richmond College, a branch of London University, and a training centre for Methodist ministers (50). It stands in eight acres of charming grounds, a relic of bygone Richmond, unsuspected by those who have not passed through the gates and seen the lawns with their tall, old trees. Before the Wesleyans owned it, it was Squire Williams's estate, and his Georgian house at the side of the College has been rebuilt, for it was blitzed in an air raid. In the early eighteenth century it was the home of George II's Court jeweller, Grose, whose son Francis, antiquarian and artist, executed a drawing of the original "Star and Garter".

The fine marble statue of John Wesley in gown and bands, a Bible in his hand, placed in the College entrance hall, was the work of Samuel Manning. The long corridor behind it leads to the new library, designed in 1931 by Edward Maufe, the architect of Guild-ford Cathedral—an ideal library, where great lamps are suspended low from the barrel-vaulted ceiling. Bays, fitted with tables and tall shelves stacked with rare books, branch from the centre aisle. Volumes, some with marginal notes, owned by the Wesley brothers, are kept in a lecture-room, and here in a glass case is Charles's autobiographical hymn-book.

Formerly the College library which had a great oriel window, was on the first floor, but Maufe replanned this apartment for use as a chapel. John Wesley's famous oak pulpit from the Old Foundry, Moorfields, London, is seen there, in a setting of deep-green and white and overhead, an azure ceiling adorned with gold stars. The stained-glass window, gentian-blue predominating in its lights, was designed by Frank Salisbury. There is an engraving in a lecture-room of Salisbury's painting of John Wesley: expressing his dissatisfaction at existing likenesses, he undertook a new one. I am told he went to a club and searched for a suitable model and the man he approached turned out to be a descendant of Charles Wesley. Another unusual portrait of John hangs in the dining-hall—the painting by Dr. Thomas Olave, Vicar of Mucking, Essex, which shows him preaching at a graveside, pointing to a skull at his feet.

Richmond was severed ecclesiastically from Kingston-upon-Thames in 1849—it will be remembered its link with that town had been forged by Gilbert the Norman in the twelfth century. The Old Vicarage on the Green replaced the Minister's little home in Church Walk, and the Charity School was moved to a new schoolhouse. These premises are still occupied by St. Mary's School. To meet the needs of the increasing population on the Hill, St. Matthias' Church was built, designed by Sir George Gilbert Scott, its 200-foot spire a notable landmark.

Scott lived for some years at the Manor House, Ham, occupied formerly by Sir Everard Home, surgeon to George III. The architect's life there was marked by a tragedy for in 1865, his son Albert Henry, home from Oxford University for the Christmas vacation, contracted a chill rowing on the river and died a few days later.

St. John's Church, at the foot of Church Road, appeared in 1831, in a setting that was then completely rural. Vulliamy, architect of many London churches, designed it in early fourteenth-century Gothic style, with a tall Decorated window over its entrance and flying buttresses. The site, like that of St. Matthias, was given by the Selwyn family: their former mansion has been replaced by Selwyn and Pagoda Avenues.

The Quadrant was not formed until 1876 and the lower part of the town was known still as World's End, and here Richmond's last ass man, John Currell, had his establishment. He advertised his steeds with these verses, believed to have been written for him by Dickens or Thackeray:

> Excellent asses' milk I sell
> And keep a stud for hire
> Of donkeys fam'd for going well
> They seldom ever tire.

One angel honour'd Balaam's ass
And met her on the way
But Currell's troops through Richmond pass
With angels every day.

Higher up by the "Bear", local laundresses used the old pound for their drying-ground. They were the best customers of the water-sellers who carried round pails of conduit water—three pails a penny—for this was considered softer than that drawn from the town's pumps.

The population of the parish of Richmond was nearly 10,000 in 1859, when the Bridge was declared toll free. The last recipient of an annuity from its first tontine was dead and the Commissioners declared its finances in good shape. At noon on March 25th, a conclave of excited townspeople marched to the toll-house and watched the removal of the gate. That night at a celebration dinner, everyone joined in the chorus of a song written to mark the great occasion and it ended with the cheerful words: "The Bridge is free! the Bridge is free!"

4

In that sentimental period when landscape gazing was a romantic pastime, when every fashionable drawing-room had albums of engraved views and a man was a hero if he had climbed from Chamonix to the Mer de Glace, the neighbourhood of Richmond attracted much attention. Everyone who was anybody, and thousands who were not, stared at some time, looking down at the serene contours of the Thames Valley from the Hill. Their sentiments were recaptured by Alaric A. Watts when he wrote:

Let poets rave of Arno's stream,
And painters of the winding Rhine,
I will not ask a lovelier dream,
A sweeter scene, fair Thames, than thine:
As 'neath a summer sun's decline,
Thou "wanderest at thine own sweet will",
Reflecting from thy face divine
The flower-wreathed brow of Richmond Hill.

"... though we had often been at Richmond for a few hours, we had no idea it was as beautiful a place as we found it on a month's acquaintance", wrote Mary Lamb to Dorothy Wordsworth in 1804. Mendelssohn drove there in a cabriolet in 1829 and passed a Sunday "quietly and solemnly", looking at the bright, warm, green land-scape, enraptured to see Windsor Castle in one direction and London in another.

At the turn of the half-century, Edward Fitzgerald, visiting his mother at the Terrace House, almost apologised in his correspon-dence for his descriptions of the scenery—the terraced gardens, the cheerful villas, the river with its decorative swans and the associations of wits and courtiers on both banks.

"Richmond", wrote Mary Russell Mitford to a friend, "is Nature in a court dress, but still Nature—aye, and very lovely nature too, gay and happy and elegant as one of Charles the Second's beauties, and with as little to remind one of the penalty of labour, or poverty, or grief, or crime. To the casual visitor (at least) Richmond appears as a sort of fairyland, a piece of old Arcadia, a holiday spot for ladies and gentlemen, where they had a happy out-of-door life, like the gay folks in Watteau's pictures, and have nothing to do with the workaday world. . . ."

Young John Ruskin sometimes drove with his parents to call on their old friend, the physician, Dr. Grant who lived on the Hill. Grant interested the boy by showing him rare specimens of minerals he had brought from South America. On these occasions they breakfasted at the "Star and Garter" and Ruskin always remembered his delight in the new French rolls. The doctor, who moved a few years later to the old Blanchard home, No. 3, the Terrace, comforted the Misses Berry in their old age, showed consideration to Barbara Hofland in her last illness.

The novelist Mrs. Hofland and her artist husband were enthusi-astic admirers of Richmond—for Hofland, ardent fisherman, it had the added attraction of being "a good angling station". They lodged frequently in the Vineyard before they settled in their last years in the Hollies in Ormond Road. He painted a fine local landscape, showing the Bridge, the Hill in the background and she produced a brave fleet of three-volume novels, of which *Son of a Genius* was the most popular. After Hofland's death in 1843, she announced in the preface to a new work that it would be her literary swansong. But habit was too strong, and, as was her custom, she continued to write after her maid had gone to bed. One night as she went upstairs, she fell and injured herself internally, although her death, three weeks later, was attributed to erysipelas. Her friends placed a memorial tablet on the south exterior wall of the Parish Church—a woman weeping over an urn with an appropriate inscription.

In the mid-nineteenth century, Prospect Lodge, near Queen Elizabeth's Almshouses in the Vineyard, was the home of the engraver, William Harvey, who had been one of Bewick's last apprentices. John Poole, dramatist and author of many comedies, produced at Richmond's Theatre Royal as well as at Drury Lane, lived for a time at Gothic House, the Green, where before the Great Exhibition of 1851, he wrote a sequel to his popular play *Paul Pry*, the meddlesome fellow whose favourite saying was, "I hope I don't intrude."

Emerson's friend, Bronson Alcott from Concord, near Boston, came to the neighbourhood in 1842, although, admittedly not to landscape gaze. He stayed at Alcott House (later South Lodge) on Ham Common, named in his honour by the socialist community who made it their centre. They invited their illustrious guest from the United States to stay with them permanently, but he returned home, taking with him their new director, Charles Long and his son. Alcott's daughter, Louisa, the author of *Little Women*, always acknowledged the benefit she derived from the lessons in essay-writing Long gave her.

The Victorian literary giants, Dickens and Thackeray, were often in the neighbourhood. One summer Dickens rented a charming Georgian house, Elm Lodge, in Petersham, and in tranquil surroundings completed a section of *Nicholas Nickleby*. The district provided him with local colour for many of his books and Richmond supplied the model for the first illustration of Mr. Pickwick. He was a plump beau, John Collins, who despite the expostulations of his lady friends, walked about the town in drab tights and black gaiters.

Thackeray praised the "Rose Cottage" Hotel in Friars Stile Road for its comfort, cleanliness and cheapness. The delightful, rustic building he knew has been replaced by the "Marlborough", but there is an adjacent tea-garden in which he may have strolled.

In September 1855, a cannon, a Crimean War trophy, was placed on the Green, where it remained the vaulting-horse of generations of children until it was removed for scrap-metal during the Second World War. (The rails and posts embossed with William IV's cypher were taken away at the same period, only a few feet being left by the verge outside Maids of Honour Row.) As soon as the cannon appeared, a quiet literary couple settled close by in No. 8, Parkshot. George Henry Lewes and Marian Evans, soon to become famous as "George Eliot", liked the little Georgian house and their friendly landlady. They shared a study and tramped in the Park, and it was during one of these walks that Lewes persuaded Marian to write fiction. *Scenes of Clerical Life* was written and *Adam Bede* took shape at No. 8, Parkshot, where Blackwood was introduced to "George Eliot". The couple lived there until February 1859.

Early this century the house, neglected, wistaria and ivy overgrown on its walls, was for sale. Some residents of Richmond, keenly aware of its literary significance, suggested that it would make an appropriate George Eliot museum. The idea was not adopted, and with two other houses, it was destroyed to make room for new premises for the Richmond Board of Guardians. They are now used by the local authorities and a tablet in the entrance hall commemorates George Eliot's achievements in Richmond.

5

Every year for a quarter of a century, on the anniversary of his wedding, Charles Dickens held a party at the "Star and Garter" Hotel, to which he alluded frequently in his letters. In June 1851, to celebrate the appearance of the last number of *David Copperfield*, he gave a banquet there and that evening, with Tennyson and Thackeray among the guests, he was in his happiest, most golden mood.

A subtle atmosphere of romance pervaded this place on the Hill.

It was said that when the black sheep of a family was at the final stage on the road to ruin, when an eligible bachelor became involved in an undesirable liaison, his footsteps turned inevitably to the "Star and Garter". The hotel featured in the most poignant scenes of Victorian fiction and even Thackeray, who sneered at it, did not ignore it in his novels.

In mid/Victorian times it was owned by Joseph Ellis and achieved a reputation for its cuisine, its choice wines. Ellis bought it from Mrs. Crean, widow of the Duke of York's cook; this landlady had charged patrons so excessively that some declared they had to pay half/a/guinea to look out of the windows. The hotel's lustre was increased by the arrival in 1848 of King Louis/Philippe and his consort, who, exiled from France, stayed there six months and were visited by Queen Victoria and Prince Albert.

That was the year that Disraeli, calling on another illustrious refugee, the Austrian statesman, Metternich, paid his well/known tribute to Richmond Green in a letter to his sister Sara: "I am enchanted with Richmond Green, which, strange to say, I don't recollect ever having visited before, often as I have been to Richmond. I should like to let my house and live there. It is still and sweet, charming alike in summer and in winter." Metternich occupied Trumpeter's House (known at this period as the Old Palace) and Disraeli thought it "the most charming house in the world", praising its library and gardens. His enthusiasm encouraged Miss Disraeli to settle in the locality and she took a house across the river at East Twickenham.

The reason why Disraeli had not discovered the Green, was because he dined as a rule with friends at the "Star and Garter". While Joseph Ellis was landlord, the hotel remained a moderate/ sized building, occupying the old house which had been added to the original tavern. Londoners who drove there on Sundays were delighted with the rural garden, its bowers of honeysuckle and jasmine. On one Sunday in 1851, five hundred dinners were served, a record at the time. It was the rendezvous of the coaching clubs, of societies of heavy intellectuals, of Bank of England directors, who realised Ellis understood wines. The American philanthropist, George Peabody, entertained sumptuously at the hotel and the *Illustrated London News* reported a banquet he gave there on Independence Day, 1856, when the dining-room was decorated with the flags of the two nations and the busts of Queen Victoria and George Washington.

Before the century was done, its visitors' book was studded with majestic names—Napoleon III and the Empress Eugénie, Queen Victoria's son-in-law, the Crown Prince of Germany, the Empress Elizabeth of Austria and Queen Isabella of Spain. Gradually its rustic touches vanished. A visitor, passing through the dining-room in 1863, a period when floral decorations superseded Georgian plate, the silver candelabra, the frosted epergne, praised the calceolarias and geraniums he noticed on the tables. "Yes, it is very nice in a small way", acknowledged the head waiter, "but if you could see the room when the dinner is three guineas a head, exclusive of wine, then it is a little heaven on earth."

The Ellis family sold the "Star and Garter" to a company in 1864, and to the existing premises, a major building was added. This, designed by E. M. Barry, resembled a French Renaissance château, its picturesque tourelles, rising like witches' hats over the Thames Valley. In 1870 the old premises were destroyed by fire and of the original building only the coffee-room remained. The ruined section was replaced by a Romanesque pavilion and aesthetes complained that the general effect was marred by three distinct styles. Another fire occurred in 1888 and swept away the historic coffee-room which, in its turn, was succeeded by an immense banqueting-hall.

But as the Victorian era closed and motor-cars carried the hotel's former patrons to fresh scenes, the decline in its prosperity was rapid. The banqueting-hall was used for social functions, but the footsteps of the great and famous no longer pattered through the corridors, the bedrooms were deserted and presently the contents were sold by auction. Shabby, locked, a hotel of gay memories, the "Star and Garter" became the White Elephant of Richmond Hill.

Chapter X

VICTORIAN DECADES

Royal Wedding at Kew—The Tecks at White Lodge—Sir Richard Owen—Lord John Russell and Pembroke Lodge—Marriage at Petersham of Miss Cecilia Nina Cavendish-Bentinck—The Terrace Gardens— Richmond becomes a Borough—Local Celebrities

I

THEY spoke of "*Our* Royal Wedding" at Kew long after that memorable summer day in 1866, when Princess Mary Adelaide of Cambridge was married to Francis, Prince of Teck, in St. Anne's Church on the Green. The parishioners, who had helped to organise preparations for the great occasion, had a close view of the important guests—the widowed Queen Victoria wore unrelieved black—and of the bride, stately in white satin and Honiton lace.

Princess Mary, daughter of Adolphus, Duke of Cambridge, had lived at Cambridge Cottage (its east wing and portico were added in 1840 and it is now Museum IV) since early child-hood. Although the local people rejoiced at her wedding, they were sad at the thought of losing "Our Princess", as they always called her.

But they saw her frequently when she came to Kew to visit her mother, for a few years after her marriage, she and the Duke of Teck resided at White Lodge in Richmond Park. In the eighteen-fifties the Lodge was the home of Mary, Duchess of Gloucester who was Ranger of the Park. (She lived, too, in the distinguished white house on Richmond Hill which bears her name: it has bows on either side of its front door, pedimented windows and a dentilled cornice.) When she died White Lodge became the home of the young Prince of Wales (the future Edward VII) before he went up to Cambridge University, and he was seen frequently rowing his boat from Richmond to Kew, on his way to visit his cousin. Queen Victoria and the Prince Consort stayed occasionally in the old mansion in the Park; after the death of the Queen's mother, the Duchess of Kent, they spent some days in complete seclusion.

The rooms Queen Victoria used were called "The Queen's Wing"; those her son occupied, "The Prince of Wales's Wing". These brick wings, originally designed by Morris for Princess Amelia, but not completed until many years later, were connected with the main Portland stone block by semicircular corridors. The Duchess of Teck's children, Princess May (Queen Mary) and her brothers, played in one wing and in the other, in later years, the Duchess had a favourite armchair.

With the exception of a few years spent on the Continent, the Tecks resided at White Lodge until almost the close of the century. When they returned from Italy, Princess May was a young woman; her boudoir, formerly Queen Victoria's sitting-room, was furnished entirely in white, its balcony overlooking a noble vista of Richmond Park. The Duchess's sanctum was the Blue Room in the Prince of Wales's Wing, and it was described by a local reporter as "a masterpiece with a blue ceiling, walls of a deeper blue and cream and gold decorations". In this room she organised her charitable activities which augmented annually.

The neighbourhood, in the final phase of its nineteenth-century development, was influenced incalculably by the Tecks. The local newspapers, *The Richmond and Twickenham Times* and *The Richmond Herald*, seldom issued a number that did not refer to their presence at social events. Balls and bazaars were given a fillip by their patronage, they attended sporting events in the Athletic Grounds, laid out in the Old Deer Park and leased from the Crown in 1886.

The Duke became the first President of the Richmond Royal Horse Show, founded by a group of townsmen in 1892. They acquired the idea when, watching a cricket match on the Green, they were impressed by the quality of the horses tethered to the railings. It developed into a recognised event of the London season, and has been held ever since: a few months after her accession, Queen Elizabeth II attended the pleasant festival of the horse her great-grandfather had helped to establish.

Noticing that the Duke of Teck always wore a flower in his lapel, a flower-seller on the Show ground offered him a cornflower, the ancient coaching emblem. He accepted it, other men followed his example, the flower and the event became inevitably associated, and now all male personnel participating in coach rides at shows in Britain wear cornflowers. The same flower-seller "buttonholed" every visitor, including the most distinguished spectators, for thirty years, and today she is replaced by nurses of the Star and Garter, who sell cornflowers for the benefit of their Home.

The Duchess of Teck and her daughter worked selflessly to expand the young Royal Hospital and the Mary Adelaide, the Cambridge and the Princess May Wards are reminders of their achievements. All that the Duchess did had a human, characteristic touch. She allowed a training-school for domestic servants at No. 4, Richmond Green, to bear her name, and every Christmas found time to attend a tea-party given to the trainees. It was held in the basement kitchens, where the Duchess, refusing to have any preparations made for her reception, sat on a hard kitchen chair and chatted to the girls as Princess May handed them cups of tea.

The Duchess never forgot the local people and before Princess May married the Duke of York (George V) in 1893, she invited them to see the wedding-presents, arranged in the corridors at White Lodge. It was anticipated that about a thousand would take advantage of her invitation: twenty thousand turned up on a wet day and the never-ending queue of umbrellas moved slowly through Richmond Park.

The following summer, on June 23rd, a Richmond physician, Dr. Wadd, joined his London colleagues at White Lodge, and after that night, he used to draw proudly from his pocket a large silver watch, which had recorded the time the new prince (the Duke of Windsor) had been born in the Prince of Wales's Wing. A cartoon appeared in the appropriate journal, depicting "Mr. Punch" approaching a cradle in White Lodge as Nurse Britannia warned, "Hush! don't wake the baby." For the last time the Richmond people turned out to welcome their Lady of the manor, Queen Victoria, as she drove from the railway station to attend the infant's christening. She was so touched by the reception she received that she knighted the Mayor who became Sir James Szlumper.

Disquieting news of the Duchess of Teck's health reached the local organisers of the Diamond Jubilee festivities. She survived the event, but with her death on October 27th, 1897, an epoch in the history of the Royal manor closed. Richmond's memorial was the red granite drinking-fountain outside the Park: a bronze plaque on one side is embossed with the Duchess's head and shoulders, the other with the symbolical figure of Charity, the quality that characterised her life. The southern light in the east window of St. Anne's, Kew, was erected by the parishioners in memory of "Our Princess", the central lights, brilliant with views of Windsor Castle and Cambridge Cottage, commemorate her parents. It seemed that the long association between Kew and the Royal family which had begun when Frederick, Prince of Wales, moved into the Capel house, had ceased when the second Duke of Cambridge died in 1904. But links in the chain have been reforged by the Marquis and Marchioness of Carisbrooke, who live in King's Cottage, once the residence of Lord Bute, and in modern times, the last home of the Archbishop of Canterbury, the late Lord Lang.

3

The Tecks had two distinguished neighbours in Richmond Park, whose homes had been granted by Queen Victoria in recognition of their public services. One was the naturalist, Professor, afterwards Sir Richard Owen, the other, the statesman, Lord John, later Earl Russell.

Owen's home, Sheen Lodge, was shattered in an air raid during the Second World War, and gone, too, is the historic Shrew Ash, which grew near it, although a sturdy shoot has sprung from it. This tree was associated with superstitious practices and in the seventeenth century, Evelyn described how mothers held their sick children beneath its boughs, believing that this act would cure them.

A stream of celebrities visited Sheen Lodge, in which Owen lived for forty years, until his death in 1892. Dickens arrived with his family—Mrs. Owen thought the beard the author had grown spoilt his appearance: Livingstone took the Professor an elephant's tusk, shaped like a corkscrew and Charles Hallé played the Sheen Lodge piano. The most eccentric caller was the mathematician,

Professor Charles Babbage. One day he sent in a piece of metal like a cogwheel, his name and the words, "No cards" scratched upon it. Owen believed that it was a fragment of Babbage's famous unfinished calculating machine.

Pembroke Lodge, the Russell home, stands on a ridge over-looking the Thames Valley. In eighteenth-century maps its site was indicated as "The Molecatchers". Elizabeth, Dowager Countess of Pembroke rented apartments in this Park servant's humble dwelling, and, taking a fancy to the spot, persuaded George III to evict the molecatcher and allow her to remain. At the end of the walk to the house from the Richmond Park Gate a recently restored board commemorates the poet James Thomson.

A winding drive leads to the Lodge, a low, long, irregular white building, altered so many times that it has no unity of plan. A small Georgian house comprises the oldest part: the second is higher and has stepped gables, and the third includes the large bow-shaped rooms the Russells occupied so happily. A meandering path over-looks the panorama of Petersham, where an extraneous landmark predominates, unknown to Lord John Russell. This is the Byzantine campanile of All Saints' Church, erected this century on the site of the former Bute estate, by the late Mrs. Lionel Warde of Peters-ham House. Its exterior is warm with Ruabon terra-cotta, its interior rich with rare materials and ornaments; its central aisle of grey and white marble was inspired by the famous one in Tournai Cathedral.

This walk leads to the King's Mount, the traditional, but most doubtful spot where Henry VIII waited to hear the Tower of London guns signal that Anne Boleyn had been executed. In a 1637 plan of the Park, it was referred to as "The King's Standinge" and it is believed to be the place where Charles I stood while deer were driven by for his marksmanship. Archaeologists state that it was an ancient barrow; these early British burial grounds have been traced in other parts of the Park.

In springtime the grounds of Pembroke Lodge, now open to the public (a restaurant has been established on the ground floor of the house) are designed with blue and mauve tapestries of wild flowers: the Russell touch is still evident in the flower-beds, lawns and little stone ornaments. Here, all the great figures of the mid-Victorian era—statesmen, artists, writers, were entertained on summer after-noons. Here, the present Lord Russell played as a boy, for after his father's death, he and his brother lived with their grandparents. On special occasions, such as Lord John's birthday, Petersham village children had tea under the cedar-tree and on the great day in 1864 when Garibaldi lunched at Pembroke Lodge, they stood in the drive to welcome him with cheers.

The Russells founded a school in Petersham in 1849, and were much amused by the protests of old residents that its innovation would destroy the aristocratic tone of the village. Classes were held in a room until 1852, and the school then built at the foot of Petersham Park served until it was destroyed in an air raid in the Second World War. It bore the founders' name but it was adopted in 1891 by the British and Foreign School Society.

Some of the Russell schoolgirls, dressed in white, bunches of daisies in their hats, scattered roses and geraniums in the path of Lord and Lady Glamis, as they left Petersham Church after their wedding in 1881. The bride, Miss Cecilia Nina Cavendish-Bentinck, destined to become the grandmother of Queen Elizabeth II, lived with her mother, Mrs. Scott, at Forbes House, Ham Common. *The Richmond and Twickenham Times* reporter recorded that she wore ivory satin trimmed with *point de gaze*, a tulle veil with orange blossom and carried a wonderful white bouquet. As she cut the wedding-cake at Forbes House, a large bell of roses which hung over her head, was swung slowly to and fro.

Queen Elizabeth the Queen Mother opened Richmond's restored Town Hall in December 1952, and recalled Forbes House as she knew it in her childhood. She referred to her grandmother's lovely garden, to the home farm and its herd of Jersey cows. Mrs. Scott's estate, which extended from Ham Common to Teddington Lock is now covered with small dwellings and the Forbes House the Queen Mother remembered has been replaced by another—an old people's home.

3

In 1881 the Countess Russell opened the Richmond Public Library on the Little Green, one of the first such institutions to be established within the area of Greater London. Many townspeople shook their heads, deplored the folly, the extravagance.

As soon as people had grown used to the new library, an historic building vanished on the other side of the Green. In 1883, the Theatre Royal, its great days long since past, was demolished (Garrick House replaced it) and with it went Kean's cottage and the trunk of an aged elm, traditionally planted by Queen Elizabeth I. The theatre properties were auctioned and some of its materials used in the construction of a local mineral water factory. Until the end of the century the "Castle" Assembly Rooms were used for dramatic performances, but in 1889 a new theatre was built by the Little Green, a Baroque-styled building with a terra-cotta façade and green "onion" caps.

The next great change came when the Vestry heard that the late Duke of Buccleuch's estate was for sale. This comprised not only the Buccleuch grounds (the land that Lady Mary Coke had remarked would be expensive to lay out), but the acres joined to them, acquired by the Duke when Lansdowne House was demolished. The trustees of the town were apprehensive—what would happen to the famous view if the site fell into the hands of a speculative builder? They purchased the ground promptly, resold the house by the river to their Member of Parliament, Sir J. Whittaker Ellis, and the Terrace Gardens were opened in May 1887, by the Duchess of Teck, representing Queen Victoria, the Lady of the Royal manor.

When we examine a contemporary drawing of the ceremony, held in a shower of rain, we see the Duchess on a stand overlooking a fountain in a basin. Made of cast iron, painted to resemble bronze, this ornament, which marked the site of the vanished Lansdowne House, had no artistic merit. Holman Hunt, Andrew Lang, George de Sala, and Burnand, the Editor of *Punch*, who lived close by in the Marlborough Road, were present at the ceremony and full of praise for the Gardens. Sir Frederic Leighton, President of the Royal Academy, who turned up late, was enraptured by the beauty of the scene, but thought the fountain "abominably hideous". He was glad to hear that it would be replaced by a more decorative ornament.

But somehow the fountain stayed there, and as the years passed, it blended unobtrusively with the delicate colouring of trees and flowers. Then during the Second World War it vanished—removed as scrap-metal.

Its subsequent replacement by a stone statue was regretted by many and caused local controversy. The Gardens, with their enchanting, elusive atmosphere, have the quality of a Fragonard painting: they form a fitting *décor* for the productions presented in them on summer nights by the local Shakespeare society. But the crude, insistent realism of a modern sculptor as a finish strikes a harsh discord. . . .

Suddenly, towards the end of the eighteen-eighties, the word "Incorporation" was on everyone's lips. The residents of the old Royal manor wished for borough status and Queen Victoria granted the Charter. On July 23rd, 1890, Charter Day, the sun shone upon the Green as the Provisional Mayor arrived from London with the document. He came in a carriage drawn by four grey horses, the postilions in pale blue jackets and white silk knee breeches. The boundaries of the new borough, fixed two years later, included Kew, Petersham and part of old Mortlake. Ham, which had had its own church since 1832, retained its own Parish Council and it was only in 1933 that the Common and some of its streets were incorporated with Richmond.

The College of Arms harked back to ancient glories when it devised the town's new badges; Henry VII's palace appeared with Tudor roses, portcullises, a lion and a swan. It was surmounted by a stag, emblematical of Royal hunts of bygone days and the motto chosen was *A Deo et Rege*. Sir J. Whittaker Ellis, first Mayor, acted as godfather and presented the old "Castle" Hotel as a site for the Town Hall, the seventeenth-century hostelry continuing to function in the Assembly Rooms. The lawn where Prince Schwarzenberg had celebrated Victoria's coronation so lavishly, was cut away from Whittaker Avenue. The vine, growing in the open air at the corner of this Avenue, which still yields grapes, had seen half a century of life when, on June 10th, 1893, the Duke of York unlocked the new Town Hall with a silver-gilt key. Then the Duke and his bride-elect, the Princess May, drove through garlanded streets to the Royal Horse Show.

The following year the Duke undertook another important local ceremony for he opened the Lock and Footbridge, spanning the river between Richmond and St. Margaret's-on-Thames. This structure, a remarkable engineering feat, was a triumph for the residents, who had persisted for years, preparing plans and models before they obtained the co-operation of the Thames Conservators. The rebuilding of London Bridge had affected the flow of the Thames and at times the silver ribbon that curved round the foot of the Hill, had looked alarmingly low. The Lock Bridge, the only one of its kind across the Thames, corrects this deficiency. Invented by Mr. F. G. Stoney of Ipswich, its three sluices, lowered when the tide ebbs, hold back the water.

That was the last outstanding local innovation of the momentous century: the final design in the Victorian pattern was woven. Noblemen no longer built elegant mansions in this Arcadia-on-Thames, but the prosperous dormitory town was beloved by many devotees of the arts. Miss Braddon and the young Maxwells still lived at Lichfield House, the dignified Queen Anne mansion in the Sheen Road (in 1892 the name of the Marsh Gate Road had been changed thus to commemorate the ancient Royal manor). The gifted novelist remained there until she died in 1915, and some years later the house was destroyed to make way for flats. Miss Rhoda Broughton, author of *Cometh up as a Flower* and *Red as a Rose is She*, occupied No. 1, Mansfield Place, on the Hill, near the hotel which still retains traces of the Countess of Mansfield's former elegant house.

No. 47, Lancaster Park was indicated as the house where pretty Miss Ramage had lived as a little girl. Her face was famous; she had been Millais's model for his popular picture "Cherry Ripe" and coloured reproductions of this hung in nurseries and kitchens throughout the land. Baby Bernard Cyril Freyberg, born at No. 8, Dynevor Road, scarcely had time to examine his native town from his perambulator before his parents whisked him away to New Zealand, of which Dominion, in the course of time, he became Governor-General.

Old Mrs. Elizabeth Evans, who lived in a cottage near the gas works in the Lower Richmond Road, grew garrulous as she repeated the harrowing tale of her experiences during the Crimean War. She had been one of the few women who had been allowed to go to the front with their soldier husbands. Mrs. Elizabeth Hanbury, the borough's celebrated centenarian, was nodding out her life in Dynevor House at the top of Mount Ararat Road. She had been a pioneer social worker, and had been associated with Elizabeth Fry's prison reforms. She died in 1901 at the age of one hundred and eight. Mr. James Walker of Ham, who had improved peach cultivation in England, was gratified to learn that some of his finest specimens had appeared on Her Majesty's table during Diamond Jubilee celebrations.

As the century died and the town band blared out "Soldiers of the Queen", Richmond's leading women collected money to assist families of Surrey's soldiers who were serving in the South African War. Difficult times . . . the town councillors sat down to their Christmas dinners realising that a stiff battle lay ahead of them, the battle for the preservation of beauty: still, they had won the first fight, for they had leased and hoped eventually to purchase Petersham Meadows from the Dysart estate. Was this so important? Yes, indeed, for it promised the continuity of the borough's greatest attraction, the treasure close to the heart of every right-minded resident—an uninterrupted view of the Thames Valley landscape from the Hill.

Chapter XI

MODERN TIMES

Star And Garter Home—Queen Elizabeth the Queen Mother reopens Town Hall—Demolition and Improvements—Twickenham Bridge—The Green

I

WHAT was to be done with the deserted "Star and Garter", hotel of myriad memories? They discussed opening it as a museum, as a winter-garden, but it was destined for a sterner, finer, purpose. In 1915 its banqueting-hall and ball-room were used as a hospital for sixty-five paralysed men of the Forces. It was recognised that a permanent home would be needed for certain types of incurable ex-servicemen, and, the hotel bought with the help of the Auctioneers and Estate Agents' Institute was presented to Queen Mary. It was hoped to reconstruct Barry's fabric, but the Victorian building proved unsuitable and funds for a new Home were collected. The women of the British Empire, adopting it as their war memorial, were generous donors, and many gave their jewels. The late Sir Edwin Cooper, R.A., was the honorary architect and King George V and Queen Mary opened it in July 1924.

The Star and Garter Home, designed in English Renaissance style, is built of roseate sandstone bricks, dressed with Portland stone. Roman tiles cover the long, steep roof and coupled Corinthian columns flank a central recess over the main entrance, enclosing a shield sculptured with the badge of the British Red Cross (51).

The entrance leads to the Memorial Hall, a splendid white shrine finished with polished Subiaco marble Ionic columns with modelled caps. The purity of the effect is intensified by the deep jewelled tones of the stained-glass windows in an apsidal recess: ruby, amber and emerald irradiate the figures in the lights designed by the late Dudley Forsyth to represent St. George, Faith and Charity, defining patriotism and sacrifice. A staircase winds to the wards, to cubicles with studied comforts, to rooms occupied by the totally incapacitated, who can never hope to leave them.

At the end of the Memorial Hall, there is a terrace walk, shaped like the letter "E" and with sheltered bays. The back of the building is finished with two more Corinthian columns, rising above a regally ornamented stone balcony. On its panel Queen Mary's profile is sculptured with fine precision, surrounded by leaves, surmounted by plumes and below, gently folded drapery—Queen Mary, as the old soldier remembers her when he was a young fellow in khaki.

The terrace overlooks a lawn, decorated with a fountain and flower-beds and enclosed on three sides by flat-roofed Doric loggias. The basement floor, opening on to a loggia, is the heart of communal activities, the focal point of the interests that enrich the lives of the men, for here are dining-room, common-rooms, library, gymnasium, cinema. Some of the amenities are provided by the Friends of the Star and Garter, a world fellowship of regular donors, for the Home does not benefit by the National Health Service. Lord Nuffield gave the workshop where men who served in the Second World War learn watchmaking: the first occupants have mastered handicrafts long ago and turned them to good account. The gold and blue chapel, its lamps designed like stars, was presented by the late Lord and Lady Cowdray, whose son perished in the First World War.

Lifts that the men can work unaided run up and down the building, lifts large enough to hold the wheel-chairs, a conspicuous feature of the Home. Wheel-chairs are turned into the Park, down the Hill into the town, and along the river. Softly their rubber tyres cross the Memorial Hall, pass out on to the terrace. Here they are brought to a standstill as their owners sit in the sun, gazing at the landscape. For the men of the Star and Garter Home have inherited the finest view of the Thames Valley, of the prospect that has enchanted millions of eyes. "*Sceone . . . syenes . . . schenes . . . schene . . .*" articulated its admirers in ancient days. And the old soldier finds it as attractive in the twentieth century as he looks down the wooded slopes, across the green meadows at the Thames, gleaming silver, now golden, winding its way into the lavender-blue

Surrey heights, the pale jade of the Berkshire downs. On a clear morning when the smoke is in abeyance, a remote, elongated speck is silhouetted against the sky. "Windsor Castle looks fine today," he says.

2

"Progress, I know, cannot be halted by sentiment, but let us be sure that it is progress and that we are not losing more than we are gaining." These wise words were spoken by Queen Elizabeth the Queen Mother on December 16th, 1952, when she reopened the Richmond Town Hall, reconstructed after its shattering in an air raid. The stripped oak decorations and the new blue leather chairs, the borough arms stamped in gold on their backs, provided a dignified setting for her black velvet and silver-fox furs, for the glittering municipal insignia, the scarlet robes of Mayor and Aldermen. Her Majesty referred to the history of the old Royal manor, to the days when she and King George VI began their married life in the tranquil surroundings of White Lodge. She urged the preservation of the fine old houses in the neighbourhood.

As the ceremony took place, three derelict buildings were being pulled down in the Sheen Road: united, they had once formed Carrington Lodge, home of the Vanderputs and later of Lord Willoughby de Broke. A few weeks before the Queen Mother's visit, a war casualty, the "Compasses" Inn vanished . . . in 1736 William Toms was threatened with amercement if he did not remove a seat he had enclosed outside "Ye Compasses", for he had encroached upon manorial land.

Yet, despite some losses, so many houses of architectural and historical interest have survived in the borough that, scheduled under the Town and Country Planning Act (1947), they provide a lengthy record. Never have they been as appreciated as they are today: the Richmond Georgian Group does good work in stimu-lating interest in the local properties of the period it indicates.

In a borough of 42,000 people, where many of the streets have remained as narrow as they were in the early nineteenth century when the population in the parish of Richmond was just above 4,000, alterations are inevitable. Sometimes they result in improvements:

the sacrifice of Buccleuch House, demolished by the Town Council in 1939, secured the continuity of the riverside walk, yielded a little garden that recalls Mary Russell Mitford's description of Richmond. Its oval lawn forms a decorative border to the immense floral tapestry behind it, the Terrace Gardens where in recent years, the horticulturist's art has found finest expression. Beyond the "Three Pigeons" the river walk is now fringed with sloping lawns, once hidden by high walls and these extend to the pearly arches of the Bridge, where the campanile of Tower House rises as it has done since the mid-nineteenth century, when it was the home of the Canadian judge and humorous writer, Thomas Chandler Haliburton, whose pen-name was "Sam Slick".

Cholmondeley Walk remains unchanged, tranquil and reminiscent of the Palace of long ago—was it here that the poet Henley thought of the verses with the lilting refrain, "Coming up from Richmond on the way to Kew"? Ahead, lies Twickenham Bridge, the fourth to span the river at Richmond, its massive concrete arches ornamented with red tiles, bronze balustrades and lamps. Maxwell Ayrton designed it and the Prince of Wales (the Duke of Windsor) opened it in 1933. It links the Chertsey Arterial Road and on the Surrey side, cuts like a white braid through the Old Deer Park. Its building was preceded by local controversy and they spoke of "The Bridge that Nobody Wants", and "The Road that leads to Nowhere", for many townsmen thought, as their eighteenth-century predecessors had done, that the new structure should link with Water Lane.

We turn up Old Palace Lane and pass on to the Green, the cradle of Richmond's history (1). It is still the "Queen's Green" for the Crown entrusts its maintenance to the local authorities, and Elizabeth II is the Lady of the Royal manor, although, of course the old manorial customs are no longer observed. Soon the cricketers will pitch their stumps close to the spot where, almost 400 years ago, Wyngaerde saw archers, the French Ambassador killed three stags outside Elizabeth I's gate, and Charles I looked at a lake of rainwater.

The almond blossom is a pink cloud in the garden of the house where Horace Walpole visited the French ladies: the paths across

the Green where Edmund Kean shivered, are dappled with
sunshine. The incidents, the figures, have taken their places in the
procession that marches into the vistas of "Time out of Mind". And
to them have been added the scenes of the Second World War,
when the old Green provided an air raid shelter, and in the eerie
lilac twilights, the town's children scuttled into its depths.

No traces remain of this war scar; never have the emerald acres
looked better. All is serene this spring afternoon. Crows build
their nests in the tall elms and old people rest in the sun as did the
Lovells, the Cockdells and the Tyes in their day. There is a
whisper in the breeze: "I am enchanted with Richmond Green. . . .
It is still and sweet, charming alike in summer and in winter."

INDEX

The numerals in heavy type refers to figure numbers of the illustrations

189

INDEX

Among trades in Richmond there is a
Sugar-plum plum — but a very small one.
The author knows so much —in "say so"
within, in short — can reach vastly
exceed his grasp